NEW YORK

BY

ERIC AND RUTH BAILEY

Produced by
Thomas Cook Publishing

Written by Eric and Ruth Bailey

Original photography by Paul Kenward

Edited and designed by Laburnum Technologies Pvt Ltd,
C-533 Triveni Apts, Sheikh Sarai Phase 1,
New Delhi 110017

Published by Thomas Cook Publishing
A division of Thomas Cook Holdings Ltd

PO Box 227, The Thomas Cook Business Park,
Units 19–21, Coningsby Road,
Peterborough PE3 8XX, United Kingdom
E-mail: books@thomascook.com
www.thomascookpublishing.com

ISBN: 1-841572-39-X

Text © 2002 Thomas Cook Publishing
Maps © 2002 Thomas Cook Publishing
First edition © 2002 Thomas Cook Publishing

Managing Director: Kevin Fitzgerald
Publisher: Donald Greig

Series Consultant: Vivien Stone

Printed and bound in Spain by: Grafo Industrias Gráficas, Basauri

Cover: Statue of Liberty, New York.
Photograph by J.Arnold/jonarnold.com
Inside cover: photographs supplied by Spectrum Colour Library

CD manufacturing services provided by business interactive ltd, Rutland, UK

C o n t e n t s

THOMAS COOK'S
NEW YORK

Introduction

Whatever your preconceived ideas of New York City – and everybody has them – there are bound to be many surprises. Some may be pleasant, like getting a friendly, chatty cab driver, but there may also be the mild shock of finding shabby commercial properties and fashionable areas side by side.

While appreciating that sophisticated Manhattan is actually hemmed in by water, visitors may not be prepared for the beautiful views of the wide Hudson and East rivers as they cross the many bridges for which the city is famous. Tunnels, too, are a feature of New York, linking the outer boroughs with Manhattan, and within the space of less than a minute you can leave one urban scene and emerge into another which is quite different. There is an area of 304 square miles to explore, much of it free, or costing no more than a few dollars.

New York's skyline was changed in a matter of moments by the terrorist attack of 11 September 2001 which brought down the soaring twin towers of the World Trade Center, but visitors will still thrill at recognising landmarks they have never seen except on the screen – the Empire State Building, the Statue of Liberty, Tiffany's, Brooklyn Bridge. And with the aid of this book, it should be easy to find a vast range of interesting, often exciting things to see and do in the world's most glamorous city.

'This is the first sensation of life in New York – you feel that the Americans have practically added a new dimension to space. They move almost as much on the perpendicular as on the horizontal plane. When they find themselves a little crowded, they simply tilt a street on end and call it a skyscraper.'
WILLIAM ARCHER, 1899

The first Cook's tour to New York took place in 1866, led by Thomas's son John Mason Cook. Thomas had visited the USA the previous year and, being a Temperance man, was impressed by American hotels, which served jugs of iced water instead of wine, and segregated drinkers and after-dinner smokers from female guests.

American tours later became a standard Thomas Cook feature; one in 1911 left from Southampton and returned 59 days later to Liverpool. Most of the tours covered the USA and Canada from coast to coast, and by 1891, Cook's had expanded to a central office in New York, at 261–262 Broadway.

'New York appears to be a great city in a great hurry. The average street pace must surely be 40 miles an hour.'
CECIL BEATON, 1938

'In the daytime Harlem looks kinda dirty, and the people a little drab and down. But at night, man, it's a swinging place, especially Spanish Harlem.'
PIRI THOMAS, 1967

'If you should happen after dark To find yourself in Central Park, Ignore the paths that beckon you And hurry, hurry to the zoo, And creep into the tiger's lair. Frankly, you'll be safer there.'
OGDEN NASH, 1947

'Something's always happening here. If you're bored in New York, it's your own fault.' **MYRNA LOY**

Studded with lights, New York City at night is a memorable sight

The City and its Suburbs

The sprawl that is New York City covers a group of islands in New York Bay, where the Hudson River enters the Atlantic Ocean. It lies at the conjunction of three states: southeastern New York, southwestern Connecticut, and northeastern New Jersey. The Narrows, a strait between Staten Island and Brooklyn, separates the upper and lower parts of the bay.

The Chrysler Building – far above the crowd

At the head of the upper bay is Manhattan Island, 13 miles long, up to 2½ miles wide, and covering 23 square miles. The island is separated from mainland America by the Hudson River to the west, the East River to the east, and the Harlem River and Spuyten Duyvil Creek in the northeast. Strictly speaking, though, the East River is a strait linking Long Island Sound and New York Bay, but it looks and smells like a river, so who is going to argue?

New York is the largest city in the USA and the core of the world's most

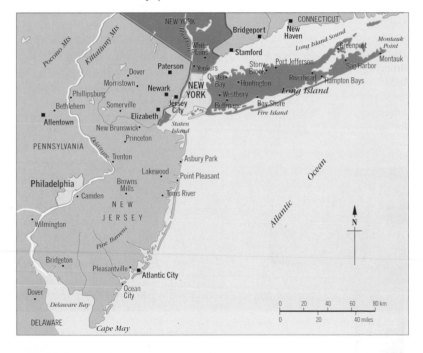

populous urbanised area. It is not, as some people think, the capital of the USA – not even of the state that also bears its name. But it is unquestionably the country's cultural, communications, corporate, and financial capital, and it takes a leading position in the fields of politics, education, industry, commerce, and transport.

The city's international stature was acknowledged after World War II when it was chosen as the site of the United Nations headquarters.

Metropolitan New York consists of five boroughs – the Bronx, Brooklyn, Manhattan, Queens, and Staten Island – covering a total of 304 square miles. Most northerly of the boroughs and the only one on the mainland, the Bronx has 2 million inhabitants, and, in the South Bronx, a fearsome reputation for violence. Settled in the 17th century by a Danish immigrant named Johannes Bronck, the Bronx today has a rich Italian heritage, splendid botanical gardens, the former homes of writers Edgar Allan Poe and Mark Twain, and, for baseball fans, the Yankee Stadium.

Brooklyn, at the western tip of Long Island, became New York's first suburb when it was annexed by the city in 1898. With more than 2½ million citizens – twice as many as Manhattan – it has cobbled streets, about 600 buildings more than a century old, and a spectacular view of Manhattan.

Queens, named to honour the wife of England's King Charles II, is the home of JF Kennedy International Airport. New Yorkers tend to think it dull, but Queens has a lively Greek community – the largest outside Greece, a South American quarter, and thriving film studios.

Staten Island is connected to Brooklyn by the 4,260-foot Verrazano-Narrows Bridge. Most visitors, however, take the 20-minute Staten Island ferry trip from Manhattan, that gives wonderful views of skyscrapers and the Statue of Liberty. The island's attractions are scattered.

Manhattan is the place where most visitors spend most of their time. Here are the famous skyscrapers, the museums, and the Broadway theatres. Here are the places known from a hundred movies.

Film scripts are hot sellers, many replaying familiar scenarios of New York City

History

1492	Columbus discovers America.
1524	Italian explorer Giovanni da Verrazano sails into New Harbor and discovers the islands that became New York City.

1609	Englishman Henry Hudson, working for the Dutch East India Company, cruises up the river that now bears his name.
1625	The Dutch establish the first permanent settlement in Lower Manhattan, named New Amsterdam.
1626	Governor Peter Minuit buys Manhattan from the Indians for trinkets worth about $24.
1636	Settlers buy what is now Brooklyn from the Indians.
1641	Johannes Bronck buys part of what is now the Bronx from the Indians, who drive settlers from Staten Island.
1643	First permanent settlement established in Flushing, Queens.
1653	New Amsterdam receives charter as municipal government. Governor Peter Stuyvesant has a wall built river-to-river to keep out British trade rivals. Where it stood is now Wall Street.

1664	The British take the city without a fight and rename it after the Duke of York, brother of King Charles II.
1673	The Dutch recapture the city and call it New Orange.
1674	The British gain permanent control of the city and province, and name both New York.
1776	After the Declaration of Independence is signed, battles take place between American and British forces. The British occupy all of what is present-day New York.
1783	Revolutionary War ends and colonies gain independence. New York becomes capital of the USA for a brief period.
1790	Census puts population of Manhattan at 33,000.
1792	Congress decides to issue stock to pay for the Revolutionary War, forming the basis of the New York Stock Exchange.
1813	Robert Fulton starts a ferry service between Manhattan and Brooklyn.
1820	Census puts population at 123,706 – New York is the nation's largest city.
1825	New York flourishes as a port. Large-scale immigration from Europe begins.
1858	Shanty-town slums in Central Manhattan are torn down to create Central Park.
1861	New York joins with 23 northern states to fight the South in the Civil War.
1883	Brooklyn Bridge opens.
1892	Beginning of the era of mass immigration through Ellis Island, where 17 million new citizens were processed into the country over 62 years.
1898	New York is officially formed with five boroughs united under one municipality – the new city is the world's second largest, with a population of 3½ million.

1902	The Flatiron Building, Madison Square, heralds the age of the skyscraper.
1920	Prohibition ushers in the age of speakeasies and gangsters.
1929	The Wall Street Crash marks the start of the Great Depression.
1931	The Empire State Building – the world's tallest at the time – is completed.
1939	Opening of LaGuardia Airport, named after hard-hitting reformist Mayor Fiorello LaGuardia.
1940	Rockefeller Center opens.
1941	Lights of Manhattan dimmed as USA enters World War II.
1952	United Nations meets at new headquarters overlooking the East River.
1973	World Trade Center opens.
1986	Statue of Liberty centenary celebrated.
1988	World Financial Center opens.
1990	New York's first black mayor, David Dinkins, takes office.
1992	Ellis Island reopens as a museum of immigration, with historical buildings restored.
1993–2001	Rudolph Giuliani elected 107th Mayor of New York City. His term ends in 2001, distinguished by a reduction in crime of almost 50%.
2001	Hillary Clinton is elected Democratic senator from New York, the first ever former First Lady to assume this political office.
11 Sep 2001	Two jet airliners smash into the twin towers of the World Trade Center, engulfing them in flames. The terrorist strike destroys the towers and several buildings in the immediate vicinity, killing approximately 5,600 people.
2002	Michael Bloomberg is elected 108th Mayor of New York City, after battling one of the most expensive election campaigns in New York's history.

Rockefeller Plaza is a business and entertainment hub in the heart of New York

Governance

Some people say New York is ungovernable, and forecasts of the city's death from fiscal failure have been made at regular intervals since the 19th century. In the 1930s, control of public services passed from the five boroughs to the mayor of New York, and since then there has been a constant, often heated, debate between the proponents of centralisation, and those who want power handed back to the boroughs.

New York City politics is a matter for personal involvement

The city's highly centralised system of government places considerable power in the hands of its mayor, who is chosen by a city-wide electorate for a term of four years.

The mayor has wide executive discretion – and a strong veto – and plays a major role in budget-making. He has the authority to organise and reorganise nine administrative agencies, including the police and fire departments, whose heads he can hire and fire.

The city comptroller, similarly elected, is another powerful figure, whose job is to recommend financial policies, and advise the mayor and city council on budget preparations.

New York's policy-making powerhouse is the Board of Estimate, which oversees the budget, as well as franchises, planning matters, public improvements, and city-owned property. The board consists of the mayor, comptroller, and president of the city council, each with two votes, and the five borough presidents who have one vote each. In 1989, the US Supreme Court ruled that this system was unconstitutional, and since then the city has been trying to develop a more acceptable way of conducting its affairs.

Calls for decentralisation have been growing stronger since the late 1960s, when fiscal problems started coming to a head as many middle-class people began to move out, and the city's tax base began to shrink. Debts mounted to $3.3 billion by 1975. A rigorous regime, involving massive cuts in services, jobs, and education, restored order by 1981.

New York is no longer as bustling as the beaver on its municipal seal might suggest. Important businesses have moved out in recent years, and many people who work in the city, using its facilities, now live and pay taxes elsewhere. Public services and amenities, and the quality of life, have certainly been downgraded since the 1960s.

Politically, the city is strongly Democrat. About 70 per cent of registered voters are said to be Democrats, and 13 per cent Republicans. There are also small Conservative and Liberal parties.

Traditionally, the mayoralty has been controlled by Democrats, but there have been times when control has passed to an alliance of other parties.

The mayoral seat has been occupied by a varied cast, some good, some rotten, many colourful. Among the most popular were Fiorello LaGuardia, nicknamed 'the Little Flower', who cracked down on crooks in a 12-year reign during the 1930s and 1940s, and Ed Koch, the no-nonsense incumbent from 1977 to 1990.

LaGuardia's background – he was a Protestant with an Italian father and a Jewish mother – served as a symbol of the mixed heritages of the citizens he subsequently led. A Republican, he was elected seven times to the US House of Representatives before turning to local government. He was elected mayor in 1933, and was the first to serve three consecutive terms. He brought about big improvements in slum clearance, public housing, and municipal amenities, flamboyantly waged war on crime and corruption – and endeared himself to New Yorkers by reading comics over the radio. Mayor Ed Koch was in many ways a latter-day LaGuardia. Elected a member of the city council in 1967, he twice served as a member of the US House of Representatives before being elected mayor. His term ended amidst a series of corruption scandals.

He was succeeded by David Dinkins, the first black mayor, and in 1993 by Rudolph Giuliani, lauded for his singular role in reducing New York's crime rate by half of what it had become. The FBI now recognises it as one of the safest large cities in America. In 2002 Michael Bloomberg, a self-made billionaire, succeeded Guiliani as mayor in what proved to be a close and costly election.

City Hall has been the backdrop for New York's controversial, turbulent, and colourful political scene

Culture

There are times in New York when 'culture' is the last word to spring to mind; yet the same city that presents some awesome scenes of human and urban dereliction, whose residents can be brutishly uncivil, is one of the greatest cultural centres on earth. New York's rich cultural diversity and its people's liberal attitudes towards the arts and education are no doubt due to standards and aspirations imported by the thousands of immigrants who poured into the city from all over the world 'yearning to be free'. New York may have been the melting pot, but the newcomers themselves were the vital ingredients that were to form its enduring cultural amalgam.

Strolling down Lexington Avenue

Until the Erie Canal opened in 1825, providing a direct link with the Great Lakes, New York was merely another slowly developing city on the Atlantic seaboard. But with goods and produce flowing to and from the American heartlands, it soon overtook Boston and Philadelphia to become the nation's major seaport. As its wealth increased, the immigrants began to arrive in ever-larger waves, bringing with them new ideas as well as new hopes. The Germans and the Irish were the first to arrive in large numbers, followed by Italians and refugees from Eastern Europe, including many Jews. In 1884 immigrants began arriving from the Near and Far East.

Each group of newcomers settled mainly with their own kind, and the city soon had recognisable ethnic communities: Chinatown and Little Italy, Jews in the Lower East Side, the Germans in Yorkville. It is a process that has continued to a large extent to the present day: the Afro-Americans in Harlem, Greeks in Astoria, Puerto Ricans in the South Bronx, and Arabs along Brooklyn's Atlantic Avenue.

Each ethnic group has had a profound effect on the city's cultural development. Music, musical comedy, the big Broadway musical show; the short story and the long novel; drama, dance, film,

Eating out in Little Italy is an authentic Italian experience

art, architecture – it all adds up to a culture not only characteristically American, but also uniquely New York.

Although New York has always been a solid enclave of capitalism, with many of its leading citizens of the past unashamedly – and sometimes ruthlessly and illegally – on the make, there have been philanthropists too, benefactors who have endowed art galleries, concert halls, museums, schools, and universities, and some of its early politicians set out to determine that in education, at least, everyone had a more or less equal chance.

To this day, New York is unique among US cities in providing public education through to university level. The City University of New York has some 175,000 students enrolled in 10 four-year and seven two-year colleges. For more than a century, university tuition was free to New York residents.

Fees were imposed only as recently as 1976, when the city found itself in deep financial trouble.

The city's Public Library, on Fifth Avenue, is one of the world's largest research libraries, with nearly 5½ million volumes and 12½ million manuscripts.

Today, New York has more theatres, concert halls, art galleries, and museums than you will find anywhere else in the USA. During the cooler months of the year, some 40 playhouses are open on Broadway, and in the West 40s and 50s streets. Off-Broadway theatres, mostly in Greenwich Village and Chelsea, number about 200.

The five boroughs are served by about 400 cinemas ranging from the Radio City Music Hall, seating up to 6,200, to small houses specialising in art films. The city has about 125 commercial art galleries, in addition to the major institutions with their world-renowned collections.

Chinatown is only one ingredient in the rich cultural mix of this city

S treet parades are a way of life in New York. Periodically, one faction or another makes its presence felt in a chunk of Fifth Avenue or some other location. The first major event after Christmas is the Chinese New Year, celebrated in January or February, on the first full moon after 19 January. Dragons, firecrackers, elaborate costumes, and the banishment of evil spirits are features of the pageantry centred on Mott Street.

The biggest procession is the St Patrick's Day Parade on 17 March. Americans claiming the merest drop of Irish blood converge from all over the nation. Manhattan bars are packed and the air is loud with pipe and brass band

music. Columbus Day, American Independence Day, Memorial and Thanksgiving Days warrant huge turnouts, too.

The Greeks celebrate their Independence Day with decorated floats in Fifth Avenue, usually in April, or in May if the day falls during the Orthodox Lent. Easter provides an excuse to parade in flamboyant, often home-made millinery. Everyone gets a generous taste of ethnic foods at the Ninth Avenue International Festival in May. Little Italy has two festivals, commemorating San Gennaro for 10 days in September, with street stalls, music, and fast food, and St Anthony of Padua for two weeks in June. Each festival involves bearing a saint's statue through the streets.

Taste of Times Square – a food festival with music and dance held on 25 June, celebrates the vibrant street life of this city. The museums have their day on 12 June when, between 6am and 9pm, the Museum Mile Festival allows visitors entry into nine museums free of charge, with plenty of outdoor music and art demonstrations for those who prefer to stay outdoors.

In late May the New Yorker Festival, a literary festival, is held at many locations, where visitors can mingle and share brunch with writers, editors, and artists. The Gay Pride Parade in June, with the accent on drag, marks the day in 1969 when a Christopher Street riot paved the way for the gay rights

movement. Ukrainians, Puerto Ricans, Germans, Hispanics, Jews, and others all have their parades and festivals, and every borough has its share of organised fun in never-a-dull-moment New York.

Facing page: St Patrick's Day parade;
Above: the Statue of Liberty, icon of New York;
Below: childhood can be magic in the city

Impressions

'New York is an ugly city, a dirty city. Its climate is a scandal, its politics are used to frighten children, its traffic is madness, its competition is murderous. But there is one thing about it – once you have lived in New York and it has become your home, no place else is good enough.'

JOHN STEINBECK, 1953

The City Layout

New York's layout is straightforward, mainly following a gridiron plan, with avenues and streets laid at right angles to each other – the avenues running north and south, and the streets east and west. Starting in the east, the avenues are numbered from First to Twelfth. Street numbers increase from south to north. On Manhattan Island, the avenues run north to south and streets east to west. The other boroughs do not have this rigid gridiron layout.

Transport

From the days of the first technicolour movies, the yellow cab has been an enduring symbol of New York City. The archetypal cab driver – laconic, lugubrious, tossing a strangled bon mot over his right shoulder as he wrestles with an oversized steering wheel – remains a monument to supreme indifference in the face of acute travel stress. 'Whaddya think this is – a helicopter?' he may sneer when you ask to be put down at Battery Park. Sometimes he may understand no more

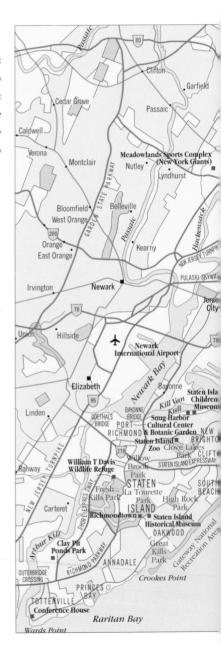

New York City

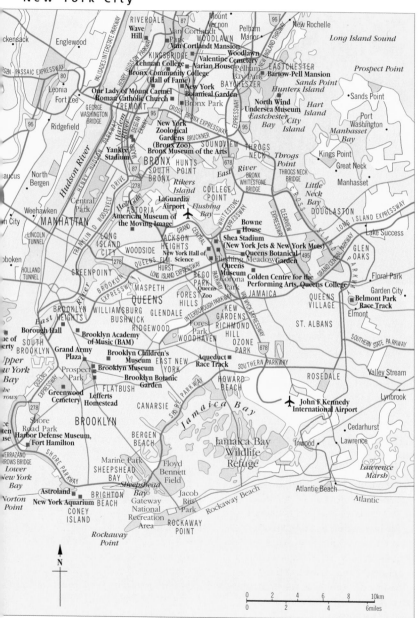

The New York subway

than a few words of English. Either way, he will expect a 15 per cent tip.

The subway, New York's 244-mile underground rail system (one of the world's most complicated underground systems), is cheap and comprehensive, but has a firmly established image of dirt and danger. Neither aspect is entirely true. The graffiti-covered trains have all but disappeared, and both plain-clothes and uniformed transit police are ubiquitous. Nevertheless, the watchword at all times is 'Be careful'.

Thanks to Manhattan's frequent traffic jams, bus travel can provide leisurely sightseeing, but you can bet your last nickel that a gridlock will occur on the dullest intersection, without a demolition or construction operation to watch, and not a cop in sight to sort things out.

Traffic jams are no problem for the Staten Island Ferry (see p126), New York's cheapest sightseeing trip – a 20-minute voyage with great views of Manhattan and New York Harbor.

Another inexpensive and exciting experience is the Roosevelt Island Aerial Tramway which crosses the East River from Second Avenue/60th Street. In the film classic *King Kong*, it was the tramway's cars that were given such a hard time by that prototype New York mugger, King Kong.

Hazard Lights

Being a pedestrian in New York can be hazardous. At intersections, illuminated signs order you to either 'Don't Walk' or 'Walk'. If it says 'Don't Walk', don't walk. If it says 'Walk', don't walk – until you have checked that you are not about to be mown down by a vehicle just behind you turning right. To prevent the city's traffic grinding to a halt even outside the rush hour – vehicles are allowed to turn into your path while you are obeying the 'Walk' sign. You need to be nimble, with a neck that swivels 360°, or very nearly.

Subway Safety

Thousands of New Yorkers use the subway every day. Others are appalled at the idea of using it at all and warn against it. Unscathed visitors sometimes wonder what the fuss is about. The subway is well policed by uniformed and plain-clothes officers. It is also a fact that the subway provides the quickest direct route between hundreds of points in Manhattan and the boroughs. And it is cheap. Take precautions. Stay with the crowd, avoid sparsely populated cars, do

Ignore these signs at your peril – walking can be a blood sport in NY

Yellow cabs lining up outside JF Kennedy International Airport

not display touristic naivety – for instance, do not peer at your map. Swot up your route in advance (for bus or subway information, *tel: (718) 330 1234.* Be alert. Do not keep your money, cheque book, or credit cards where an opportunist can grab them. Wear your shoulder bag with the fastening against your body. Men should not strap-hang with their jackets gaping open revealing a wallet. It may be wise to use surface transport at night. Just be as sensible as you would be in a similar situation at home.

Bridges and Tunnels
The East River separates Manhattan from Queens and Brooklyn. The Harlem River separates Manhattan from the

The boys in blue – New York's cops lead the city's ongoing fight against crime

Bronx. The Hudson River separates Manhattan from New Jersey which, although a different state, provides Manhattan with much of its workforce. Consequently, New York City has more than 60 bridges. Circle Line's 35-mile cruise around Manhattan Island passes under 20 of them and through four tunnels and 73 transit subways.

Recognising the snob appeal of Manhattan, residents have a tendency to demonstrate superiority to New Yorkers from the other boroughs, referring to them as Bridge and Tunnel people. The beauty of **Brooklyn Bridge** is universally admired. It spans the East River and was regarded as the Eighth Wonder of the World when it opened in 1883. It was the world's first steel suspension bridge, hanging between two 268-foot towers and supported by steel wire cables. The work, led by John Roebling and his son, took 15 years.

In 1964, the 4,260-foot **Verrazano-**

Visitors should take time to accustom themselves to the distinctive city layout

Narrows Bridge was completed – for a time the world's longest suspension bridge. It links Staten Island with Brooklyn, and is named after the Italian explorer Giovanni da Verrazano who, in 1524, was the first white man to see what later became New York.

Manhattan Bridge, which leads off Canal Street to cross the East River to Brooklyn, has a much-ornamented archway.

Tolls are payable on many of the bridges and tunnels. Charges for some are payable in one direction only. For example, there is a fee for a car crossing the Verrazano-Narrows Bridge westward from Brooklyn to Staten Island, but the journey in the opposite direction is free. Drivers of cars using **Midtown Tunnel** or the **Triborough Bridge**, both of

The George Washington Bridge

The pedestrian walkway across Brooklyn Bridge provides a close-up view of this engineering marvel

Many New Yorkers prefer to commute by cab

which link Long Island with Manhattan, must pay a toll in each direction.

Two tunnels and a bridge carry traffic over or under the Hudson River between New Jersey and Manhattan. The **George Washington Bridge**, opened in 1931 and transporting 14 lanes of traffic, goes into the north of the borough at West 178th Street, making a graceful and sweeping connection between the neighbouring states.

The **Lincoln Tunnel** enters Manhattan at Midtown. The **Holland Tunnel** goes into Lower Manhattan, emerging at the western end of Canal Street. With Manhattan Bridge (no toll) at Canal Street's eastern end, it provides a direct connection between New Jersey

and Long Island. A toll is charged on each of these three links for cars travelling east to Manhattan. There is no toll for westbound traffic.

Near Triborough Bridge, just north of **Hell Gate Bridge**, looking towards Ward Island and Randall's Island, the turbulence at the meeting of the East River, Long Island Sound, and Harlem River is much in evidence.

Queensborough Bridge, opened in 1909, has a 7,000-foot span. It goes over the East River from East 60th Street, Manhattan, to Crescent Street, Queens, crossing Roosevelt Island. Although Roosevelt Island is mainly residential, with little of interest to see, many people make the crossing on Roosevelt Island Aerial Tramway just for the fun of it. This is a horizontal cable car system, which goes between 60th Street at Second Avenue and the island, following the line of Queensborough Bridge. The journey takes less than four minutes, providing great views, and currently costs $1.50 in each direction.

At Murray Hill, the **Queens-Midtown Tunnel**, with entrances between First and Second Avenues around 38th Street, goes under the East River to Queens.

The model of the five boroughs at Queens Museum in Flushing Meadow illustrates how dependent New York City is on its bridges and tunnels.

What Makes New Yorkers Tick?

Like most Americans, New Yorkers are extremely articulate. But on a superficial level, when making comments to strangers, for example, they tend to be monosyllabic, delivering one-liners, or making the odd wisecrack straight-faced. It may sound blunt, but do not read it as unfriendly. These are not over-effusive people.

The USA is as close as you can get to a classless society. Those serving you may be tomorrow's tycoons, yesterday's recession-hit graduates, or today's workforce making a career in the vital hospitality industry.

However, while New Yorkers may not be class-conscious, in so far as it does not matter to them how your father earned a living, you should observe the concept that money talks, and bet your bottom dollar they are listening.

Most people in New York have either a positive or negative attitude towards drink. The trouble is, you do not know which it is until you have a large dry gin in your hand. 'Time for cocktails. We deserve it,' they say, leading you to the

Detail of George Washington Bridge

bar. Once your guilty pick-me-up is delivered, they may put you down by ordering themselves a Perrier or tomato juice.

It is only a form of one-upmanship. Enjoy your drink, and consider yourself one up on them!

Fireworks light up the New York skyline

The ferry on the way to or from Staten Island provides a good view of New York Harbor, discovered in 1524 by Italian explorer Giovanni da Verrazano who sailed into the natural harbour within which nestled the islands that were to form New York City. It was the Dutch who first established a permanent settlement in lower Manhattan, but the harbour was too valuable an asset to be acquired so peacefully. Skirmishes to win ownership continued until the British gained control in 1674.

Over the years, a virtual sea of humanity has crossed the harbour into the mainland. To the many Africans who encountered it, it was just a frightening, floating stop on an arduous nightmare journey. There was a slave market on Wall Street. To others, it was the gateway to opportunity. More than 17 million immigrants disembarked here, mainly from Europe, to be processed and accepted as New Americans. Some were attracted by the wide expanses of the hinterland, but many chose to settle in the city, endowing it with its characteristic mix of cultures.

Seeing the harbour from the water gives a different perspective – the dramatic view of the Statue of Liberty against the backdrop of the Manhattan skyline is truly memorable, and gives the few who arrive by sea an advantage over the masses who now arrive by air.

Airline passengers, however, do get a bird's-eye glimpse of the geography of the harbour, with its narrow bottleneck between the open Atlantic Ocean and the almost landlocked haven into which

Circle Line cruises
take in all the
harbour views

the Hudson River flows after its 306-mile journey. The river occupies a deep underwater canyon that provides good deep-water facilities for ocean-going ships entering Manhattan.

Ferries go to Staten Island, Ellis Island, and Liberty Island. Circle Line cruises and World Yacht luncheon and dinner cruises, operated by New York Cruise Lines, provide an opportunity to view the city's spectacular skyline and some of its famous landmarks from the surrounding waterways. In the evening, the company runs Harbor Lights cruises.

Across the narrow mouth of the harbour is the elegant Verrazano-Narrows Bridge, linking Staten Island and Brooklyn. At 4,260 feet, it was the longest bridge in the world when it opened in 1964. The Hudson River is 4,000 feet wide in its lower reaches, separating New York from New Jersey.

Among the sights seen by passengers on the 35-mile trip around Manhattan Island are the Financial District landmarks – the World Financial Center, the New Jersey Palisades, and the George Washington Bridge.

Manhattan

More than 1½ million people live in Manhattan, which has evolved over the past 400 years and is continually changing. The island measures approximately 13½ miles long by 2¼ miles wide at the widest point – less than 1 mile at its narrowest. Apart from the great green rectangle which is Central Park, it is almost all covered in buildings and roads.

Fifth Avenue is one of the most stylish addresses

Nothing could be simpler than the geography of Manhattan. The borough is divided into three major districts: Downtown, Midtown, and Upper Manhattan. Downtown is the most southerly area, generally agreed to extend as far north as 23rd Street. Midtown goes up to Central Park, and everywhere else is Upper Manhattan.

Downtown is where the grid pattern falls to bits. This was the first area of Manhattan to be settled, so its streets tend to follow the customs of the Old World, and have names rather than numbers.

Movement across the city is 'uptown', 'downtown', or 'crosstown'. Anywhere north of a given location is uptown; downtown is to the south, and crosstown is east or west.

Avenues run from First on the East River to 12th on the Hudson River. There are some inconsistencies. Lexington, Park, and Madison Avenues run between Third and Fifth Avenues. Fourth Avenue is a short downtown stretch extending from the Bowery to East 14th Street. Sixth Avenue is officially known as the Avenue of the Americas.

Broadway is the wild card, running straight from Bowling Green to East 10th Street where it suddenly kinks westwards to West 79th Street.

In the Upper East Side, York Avenue runs between First Avenue and the East River. In the Lower East Side is Alphabet City – Avenues A, B, C, and D lying between First Avenue and Roosevelt Parkway.

Before you start to explore the borough, you may like to sample one or more ways of getting an introductory perspective on Manhattan. There are two useful and pleasurable ways of doing this. One is to take the three-hour, 35-mile Circle Line cruise around the island (*see p185*).

The second option is to cross the East River to Queens. In Flushing Meadow/Corona Park is the Queens Museum, which contains a constantly updated model of the five boroughs.

Abigail Adams Smith Museum

A 1799 carriage house, converted into a country hotel in 1826, is now a museum of 19th-century New York City history and decorative arts. There are guided tours of period rooms.

421 E 61st St. Tel: (212) 838 6878.
Open: Tue–Sun noon–4pm.
Closed: holidays & through Aug.
Admission charge. Subway: 59th St.

American Bible Society (Bible House)

Rare historic Bibles, unusual current
editions in English and other languages,
and the Dead Sea scrolls are among the
exhibits.
1865 Broadway/61st St, near Lincoln
Center. Tel: (212) 408 1200. Open: Mon,
Wed, Thu 10am–6pm, Sat 10am–5pm.
Free admission. Subway: 59th St.

American Craft Museum

The nation's premier showcase for
contemporary craft presents exhibitions
of quilts, jewellery, rugs, architectural
ceramics, art-to-wear, handmade paper,
woodware, and other crafts. Special
'Meet the Artist' programmes are
arranged. The permanent collection
demonstrates the emergence of the US
craft movement since World War II.
40 W 53rd St. Tel: (212) 956 3535.
Open: Tue 10am–8pm, Wed–Sun
10am–6pm, Thu 10am–8pm. Admission
charge. Subway: 5th Ave/W 53rd St.

American Museum of Natural History/Rose Planetarium

Permanent exhibitions in different halls
are devoted to the peoples of Asia, South
America, the Pacific and Africa, Mexico,
Central America, and to American
Indians. There are also sections on
dinosaurs, minerals and meteorites,
gems, molluscs, African and Asian
animals and birds. The museum houses
a collection of some 36 million artefacts
– surely something for everyone.

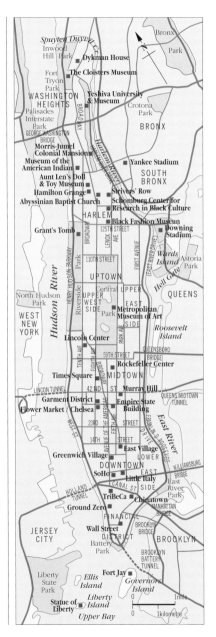

There is a calendar of frequent special events, and a Naturemax Theater with a screen four storeys high.

The Planetarium has the Space Theater, computerised special effects, and live shows for children on some Saturday mornings.

Central Park West/E 79th St. Tel: (212) 769 5100. Open: Sun–Thu 10am– 5.45pm, Fri & Sat 10am–8.45pm. Closed: Thanksgiving & Christmas Day. Museum: free admission on Fri & Sat evenings, donation suggested at other times (admission charge for Naturemax Theater).

Planetarium: admission charge, extra charge for laser light shows held on Fri & Sat. Access from museum first floor or at separate entrance, Central Park West/81st St. Tel: (212) 769 5200. Open: see American Museum of Natural History for times. Subway: 81st St/Central Park West.

American Numismatic Society

Coins, medals, and decorations from many countries are displayed.

Broadway/155th St. Tel: (212) 234 3130. Open: Tue–Fri 9am–4.30pm. Free admission. Subway: 157th St.

Americas Society

Exhibitions from Central and South America, Canada, and the Caribbean.

680 Park Ave/68th St. Tel: (212) 249 8950. Open: Tue–Sun noon–6pm. Free admission. Subway: E 68th St.

Asia Society

The Society's dynamic programme of activities has recently been accommodated in a new interior design that doubles the original space for John D

The magnificent window in St John the Divine

Rockefeller's Asian art collection.

725 Park Ave/70th St. Tel: (212) 288 6400. Open: Tue–Sat 10am–6pm, Fri till 9pm. Gallery tours: Tue–Sat 12.30pm. Subway: E 68th St.

Battery Park

This green esplanade overlooks New York Harbor, Staten Island, Liberty Island, and Governor's Island. Established in 1870 from 22 acres of landfill, it is named after the battery of cannons lined around the shore. (*See pp90–91.*)

Lower Manhattan. Subway: Bowling Green.

Brooklyn Bridge

One of the great engineering feats of the 19th century, and the first suspension bridge made of steel cables, it is still considered by many to be the most beautiful bridge in the world. Before it opened in 1883, the only way across the East River was by ferry. The view of Manhattan from the pedestrian walkway is spectacular, especially at night.

Lower Manhattan. Subway: Brooklyn Bridge/City Hall.

Carnegie Hall

This opera and concert venue celebrated its centenary during the 1990–91 season. It was opened in 1891, when Tchaikovsky travelled from Russia for the first concert. Since then, many of the world's leading performers have packed the hall, among them Mahler, Caruso, Toscanini, Leonard Bernstein, Frank Sinatra, and the Beatles. Some of the nation's greatest symphony orchestras have regular seasons here. Carnegie Hall, which seats nearly 2,800, and the Weill Recital Hall, with a capacity of 270, both on an upper floor, underwent major renovation in 1986.
154 W 57th St. Tel: (212) 247 7800.
Open: Mon, Tue, Thu, & Fri 11.30am,
2pm, & 3pm. Admission charge for guided
tours. Tel: (212) 903 9790.
Subway: 7th Ave/57th St.

Castle Clinton National Monument

The fort was built to defend New York Harbor during the war of 1812. It became an entertainment centre called Castle Garden in 1824, then an immigration depot. About 8 million people entered the USA through Castle Clinton between 1855 and 1890. Later it became a popular aquarium. It was given national monument status in 1946, and now contains a museum depicting its past. Tickets for the Statue of Liberty ferry are sold here.
Battery Park. Tel: (212) 344 7220.
Open: daily 9am–5pm. Free admission.
Subway: Bowling Green.

Cathedral Church of St John the Divine

Begun in 1892 and still under construction, the church seems destined to be the world's largest Neo-Gothic cathedral. The nave alone will be twice as big as a full-size American football pitch, seating 5,000 people. The Episcopal cathedral stands in 13 acres, and has a shelter for the homeless, a gymnasium, biblical garden, museum of religious art, and a gift shop. Art exhibitions and free concerts are also held in addition to regular services and special events. Specially trained stone cutters, drawn from the local community, can be seen at work as the cathedral is supported in traditional style by stonemasonry, rather than today's steel framework. Despite a fire in December 2001, the church is open, with a lively programme of activities.
1047 Amsterdam Ave/112th St.
Tel: (212) 932 7314. Open: Mon–Sat
7am–6pm, Sun 7am–8pm. Tours: Tue–
Sat 11am; Sun 1pm.
Subway: 110th St/Cathedral Parkway.

Carnegie Hall is at the centre of New York's musical life

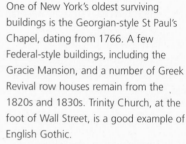

Anyone with the eye to recognise it, can trace New York's modern history through its architecture – in some cases thanks to civic preservationists of the past. There were moves at one time, for example, to pull down most of seedy SoHo. The warehouses here and in neighbouring TriBeCa were saved by the noisy insistence of enough persuasive people to influence the planners. The vast lofts of the sweatshops became fashionable homes and studios for artists, and industrial buildings became gracious residences.

One of New York's oldest surviving buildings is the Georgian-style St Paul's Chapel, dating from 1766. A few Federal-style buildings, including the Gracie Mansion, and a number of Greek Revival row houses remain from the 1820s and 1830s. Trinity Church, at the foot of Wall Street, is a good example of English Gothic.

New Yorkers are justifiably proud of their striking brownstone houses. Brownstone, quarried in Connecticut, first appeared in the 1840s as a façade on Neo-Gothic and Italianate town houses, and was used in such profusion

– thousands of brownstones were built in Manhattan and Brooklyn – that one critic dismissed it as 'chocolate sauce'.

It was, however, the introduction of 19th-century technology – cast-iron façades – that had the biggest impact on the city's architecture. Although lighter, its stronger method of construction enabled buildings to grow skywards, and to carry much classical ornamentation.

New York's first skyscraper was the triangular Flatiron Building, which went up early in the 1900s on Madison Square. By 1913, the 60-storey Woolworth

Building on Broadway was hailed as the world's tallest. It was overshadowed by the quarter-mile high twin towers of the 1973 World Trade Center, until the September 2001 terrorist attacks brought them down. As sky-high buildings formed canyons in Midtown and Lower Manhattan, rules were imposed requiring buildings to be 'tiered' after a certain height to let the light in, lending them the flavour of the Art Deco style.

Seen from the air, the jumble of high-rises that comprise New York does not reveal the character of individual buildings such as the Flatiron building (facing page) and Woolworth Building (right)

O nce, there was only Broadway – that Great White Way of some 50 theatres clustered in the Times Square area. Here was the pre-war world of glamour and glitter, with big names in bright lights, and more stars on stage than you could see in Manhattan's night sky. Then came Off-Broadway, a shadowy outer ring of lowlier playhouses, lesser players, and cheaper tickets. Off-Off-Broadway was further out in every sense. But then the scene changed. Many of the old Broadway houses vanished in clouds of demolition dust, the Theater District extended west to Ninth Avenue and north to 53rd Street, and demarcation lines became blurred as standards rose and new talents emerged. The fact that a performance takes place in an Off-Broadway location does not necessarily mean that the audience will be sitting in dusty bargain seats, watching a show in which the prompt is busier than the players. The Off- or even Off-Off-Broadway show of today may be the smash hit of tomorrow. It may miss out Broadway altogether, and go on to conquer the world. It has happened before. Indeed, these experimental theatre productions, staged in anything from a one-bulb garage to a converted church, are the very best in the world.

Nostalgia nevertheless rules along the Great White Way, and echoes of the past can still be heard in the wings, orchestra pits, and dressing rooms of the few theatres still surviving

from those heady pre-TV days. The St James, at 246 W 44th Street, saw Lauren Bacall begin her Broadway career in the 1940s – as an usherette. Barbra Streisand took her first bow at the Schubert Theater, 225 W 44th Street, where
A Chorus Line ran for a record-breaking 15 years. Among historic productions staged, since 1924, at the Martin Beck Theater, 302 W 45th Street, was the premiere of Eugene O'Neill's *The Iceman Cometh*.

Broadway gave the musical to the world – and the Great White Way remains synonymous with all the gloss and the glamour of high-quality showmanship

The spire of the Chrysler Building is instantly identifiable in the New York skyline

Central Park
See pp38–41.

Central Park Zoo
Wildlife from polar, temperate, and tropical zones is housed in uncaged habitats. More than 400 animals and birds from around 100 species are represented here. Nearby is a children's petting zoo.
E 64th St/5th Ave. Tel: (212) 861 6030. Open: weekdays 10am–5pm, weekends & holidays 10.30am–5.30pm; Nov–Mar, daily 10am–4.30pm. Admission charge. Subway: 68th St/Hunter College Station.

Children's Museum of Manhattan
The multi-media show in the 'Brainatorium' demonstrates how the brain works. Nature, art, and science are all presented entertainingly. There is a hands-on media centre and TV studio, as well as programmes for pre-school children. Dancing, music, theatre, and storytelling sessions and workshops are held at weekends and during holidays.
Tisch Building, 212 W 83rd St. Tel: (212) 721 1234. Open: Wed–Sun & on school holidays 10am–5pm. Admission charge; extra for performances and workshops. Subway: 81st St/Central Park West.

Chinatown
See Walk pp42–3.

Chrysler Building
An outstanding skyscraper in Art Deco architecture, it was briefly the world's tallest building until the Empire State Building went up in 1931. Its unusual stainless steel scaled spire, illuminated at night, makes it a familiar part of the New York skyline. Visitors are permitted only into the lobby, which has African marble walls. Ceiling murals depict workers constructing the spire. In the building is the Con Edison's Conservation Center, with hands-on exhibits, energy-saving and money-saving ideas, and experts at hand to answer questions on conservation.
At the corner of 405 Lexington Ave/42nd St. Tel: (212) 682 3070. Conservation Center closed Sun & Mon. Free admission. Subway: Grand Central Station.

Church of the Transfiguration
A John La Farge stained-glass window shows 19th-century actor Edwin Booth as Hamlet. Actors, writers, and show business people are among the worshippers here, and the church sponsors a small acting company. (Chinatown also has a Church of the Transfiguration in Mott Street. Opened in 1801 as a Lutheran Zion church, it is now used by Asian Roman Catholics.)

1 E 29th St. Tel: (212) 684 6770.
Subway: Park Ave/28th St.

Citicorp Center

Completed in 1979, this is an eye-catching building with a sharply sloping roof, intended for a solar energy project that was never completed. Amongst the world's tallest buildings, it has a three-level mall of shops and restaurants surrounding a skylit atrium known as The Market. Live music is played at weekends. At street level is
St Peter's, a small modern church, with Wednesday lunchtime jazz concerts.
Lexington Ave/153 E 53rd St.
Tel: (212) 559 2209. Open: daily.
Subway: Lexington/3rd aves.

City Hall

The seat of New York's municipal government since 1811 this is an outstanding example of Federal period architecture. This is a landmark building which some have described as the most beautiful in the USA. It is elegant from its frontal columns to its cupola, topped with a figure of Lady Justice. The Mayor's office is on the ground floor. What used to be the governor's office has become a museum and portrait gallery.
City Hall Park, Broadway/Murray St.
Tel: (212) 788 6879.
Open: Mon–Fri 9am–4pm.
Free admission.
Subway: City Hall/Broadway.

Lunchtime break in City Hall Park

Central Park

Baseball in Central Park

A placid, green rectangle set among the crazed order of city streets, Central Park covers a surprisingly large area – 843 acres of land that must cause nightmares for property developers working out its worth in terms of the rent they could charge for each square foot. In the 1850s, however, there were doubts about the city's wisdom in purchasing a precinct of rocks, swamp, and shanty town at what was then the exorbitant price of $7,500 an acre.

The idea of creating a central reserve of grass, trees, and tranquillity for the rapidly growing city was first voiced in 1844 by poet and journalist William Cullen Bryant, but it took many years to persuade the authorities not to give in to the demands of developers.

Finally, a competition was staged to find the best plan for the park, and the winners – landscape designer Frederick Law Olmsted and architect Calvert Vaux – started the construction work in 1860.

It took Olmsted and Vaux 16 years to accomplish their dream of creating a bucolic Valhalla in the middle of what was already one of the world's greatest cities, to say nothing of $14 million and the shifting around of some 5 million cubic yards of earth and rock.

Their achievement in transforming an area of near-wilderness into rolling countryside, with thick woodlands, lakes, and lawns – even farm buildings and a meadow on which sheep really did graze – was widely acclaimed, and they were commissioned to create landscapes in other parts of the USA, including Capitol Hill in Washington DC.

The stroke of genius in the scheme drawn up by Olmsted and Vaux was the creation of transverse roads which passed underneath a meandering network of footpaths, enabling through-traffic to cross the park without disturbing the peace of visitors.

Central Park's layout today is much the same as its designers intended. Acts of civic vandalism, which turned areas of greenery into hard-surfaced playgrounds and fenced-off games pitches, have been mitigated to some extent since 1980, by extensive restoration.

Despite its reputation as a haunt of muggers and junkies, the park has the city's lowest crime rate – policing has been increased dramatically in recent years – and its popularity is obvious, especially during summer weekends when people turn out in their hundreds. Even in the depths of winter, it takes no more than a light fall of overnight snow to bring out the sledges and skis.

Summer or winter, the southern quarter of the park is the place for family fun. Here, within a few minutes' walk of Columbus Circle or Grand

Army Plaza, you can have the kites and frisbees flying, get your skates on, sunbathe, or visit the zoo animals.

Information about the park can be obtained from the Dairy, while just north of here, the Sheep Meadow is a popular place for picnics and free concerts on summer evenings. Further north still, bikes and boats can be rented at the Loeb Boathouse, and Shakespeare is performed at the Delacorte Theater. Nearby, the Shakespeare Garden is filled with plants mentioned by the Bard.

Another favourite picnic area for the crowds is the Great Lawn, parallel with the Metropolitan Museum of Art. Above this is the Reservoir, more often than not ringed with joggers.

Less popular and, therefore, quieter, is the northern quarter, with its pools and three formal gardens donated by the wealthy Vanderbilt family.

A pause for refreshment

An oasis ringed by sentinel skyscrapers

Walk: Central Park

Central Park is much larger than it seems – almost 850 acres of lawns, lakes, and woodlands, where visitors can follow pursuits as diverse as skating and birdwatching, jogging and croquet, cycling, or simply sitting still. *Allow 2 hours.*

Begin at W 72nd St subway station, cross Central Park West and West Drive, and follow the path to Strawberry Fields.

1 Strawberry Fields

This hillside garden is dedicated to John Lennon, murdered in December 1980 outside the Dakota Building just across Central Park West. Lennon's wife, Yoko Ono, still lives at the Dakota, and the Strawberry Fields site is maintained through an endowment she has made.
Head north, following either of the paths skirting West Drive (the lakeside one is best), then turn right on to the path on the north side of the 79th St Transverse.

2 Cottage and Castle

The wooden chalet is the Swedish Cottage, one of the park's many architectural oddities. Another is the nearby Belvedere Castle, a whimsical amalgam of medieval styles built in 1872 to enhance the view from across the Lake. The castle itself affords a view of the Delacorte Theater and the park's Great Lawn beyond.

Between cottage and castle is the Shakespeare Garden, with plants mentioned in the Bard's works.
Continue east, crossing the intersection of 79th St Transverse and East Drive. Take the path south to Conservatory Water.

3 Conservatory Water

Remote-control model boats compete in exciting races on Saturday mornings in summer; it is a pleasant spot at any

The John Lennon Memorial

time. Children can climb all over Lewis Carroll's Alice and the other Wonderland characters in the bronze sculpture at the northern end of the pond, or listen to tales being told at the foot of a statue of Hans Christian Andersen on the west side.

Head west along the path that crosses East Drive and leads to the Loeb Boathouse.

4 The Lake

Rowboats and gondolas (and bikes) can be rented at the Loeb Boathouse, which also has a reasonable restaurant. Exercise apart, the lake provides an excellent foreground for photographs, paintings, or sketches of New York's various profiles. A good place is the cast-iron Bow Bridge, which crosses the narrow neck of water between the smaller and larger sections of the Lake. Midway between boathouse and bridge, the Bethesda Fountain, set on a strikingly paved terrace, provides further photographic opportunities.

From the fountain take the tiled tunnel south to pass under the 72nd St Transverse and reach The Mall.

5 The Mall

At the northern end of The Mall is the Bandshell, where summer concerts and other performances take place. The Mall itself, some 300 yards long, is known as the 'Literary Walk' because it is also lined with the statues of world-famous writers. West of The Mall, is Sheep Meadow, 15 acres of open space in which anything noisier or more energetic than picnicking is banned.

At the foot of The Mall, cross to the western side of East Drive.

6 Southeast Corner

Just below the 65th Street Transverse is the Dairy, now used as the park's visitor centre. South of the Dairy is the **Wollman Memorial Rink**, where New Yorkers skate. This corner of the park is taken up by the often photographed Pond.

Follow the path to the Pond's southern edge and turn left to complete the walk at Grand Army Plaza.

Cleopatra's Needle, the Great Lawn, and the Metropolitan Museum of Art are some other sights on this walk.

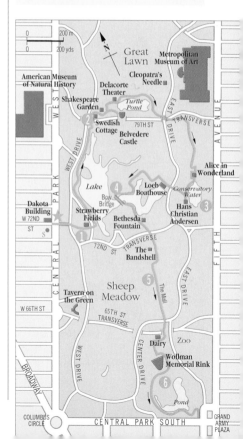

Walk: Chinatown

Settled by early 20th-century immigrants from China, this is a vibrant enclave. Once in Chinatown, it is easy to be sidetracked as food shops, restaurants, coffee houses, Buddhist temples, and little bazaars command attention. *Allow 1½ hours.*

Begin at the junction of Bowery and Canal St (nearest subway station is Grand St, two blocks north). Notice the dome of the old Police Headquarters to the right, behind you. Turn south down Bowery.

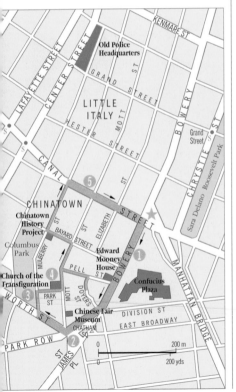

1 Bowery

Not Manhattan's most salubrious thoroughfare, Bowery was once the scene of popular musical and theatrical entertainment. Today, all this has gone, and down-and-outs live rough on the street. Confucius Plaza at 19 Bowery has a statue of the Chinese philosopher in front of a modern residential development. On the corner of Pell Street, at 18 Bowery, is Edward Mooney House, the oldest known town house surviving in Manhattan. Built about 1789, it was originally the home of a wealthy meat merchant who bred racehorses. In modern times it has been, amongst other things, a betting parlour. *Continue south along Bowery to Chatham Square.*

2 Chatham Square

This lies at the intersection of 10 streets, and is as much a hazard for pedestrians as it is for motor traffic. Chinese victims of American wars are honoured by an Oriental memorial arch in the centre of the square. On the east side at East Broadway is a pagoda-style building housing a bank. *At the southwest corner of Chatham Square turn into Worth St, then right into Mulberry St.*

3 Mulberry Street

On the left you will see Columbus Park, formerly an immigrant slum area. Mulberry Street extends north into Little Italy. Canal Street once marked the boundary between Little Italy and Chinatown, but Asians have gradually spread into the area. At No. 70, on the corner of Bayard Street, is the Chinatown History Project, with photographs tracing the history of Southeast Asians in America.
Turn right into Park St then left into Mott St.

4 Mott Street

Dominating the corner of Mott and Park streets is the imposing Church of the Transfiguration, built early in the 19th century, where the Chinese Catholics worship. It was originally the Zion Episcopal Church. At No. 8 Mott Street is the Chinese Fair Amusement Arcade and Museum. Mott Street, the lively, teeming heart of New York's Chinatown, is the place to buy bargain kitchenware, chopsticks, and woks, as well as Mandarin, Shanghai, Cantonese, Hunan, Szechuan, Vietnamese, and other Far Eastern cuisines. Ingredients for many Oriental dishes can also be found here, and there are good selections of Eastern souvenirs, such as jade ornaments and silks. Take a look along narrow Pell Street and Doyers Street, which leads off it. The corner of these streets used to be called 'The Bloody Angle' – bodies of men killed in the Tong (clan association) Wars were often dumped here. On the brighter side, this area is where revelries are focused during the Chinese New Year,

A lively, bustling enclave

celebrated at the first full moon after 19 January. Traditional Chinese dragons parade through the streets, firework displays ward off evil spirits, and martial arts are deftly demonstrated.
Return to Mott St. Turn right, then left at Bayard St, right into Mulberry St, and right into Canal St.

5 Canal Street

Like Bayard Street, Canal Street has food stalls piled high with herbs, Chinese mushrooms, bean curd, snow peas, dried fungi, fresh seafood, and exotic fruit and vegetables. There are also clothing discount stores, shops selling electrical goods, and the enticing Kam Man supermarket. Originally a drainage waterway, from which it took its name, Canal Street links the Holland Tunnel in the west with Manhattan Bridge in the east, and provides a continuous connection between New Jersey and Long Island. A short walk eastwards takes you back to Confucius Plaza.
Continue a few yards along Canal St for a view to the right of the Manhattan Bridge, with its central triumphal arch.

Churches

Cathedral of St John the Divine

When finished, the construction of this Episcopal cathedral will have spanned three centuries. It was started in 1892 in Romanesque style, but also has Gothic and medieval elements. Work was interrupted by World War II and was not resumed until 1982. It is expected to be completed by the mid-21st century, with floorspace equal to two American football pitches, making it the world's biggest cathedral. Daily tours are conducted. The grounds include a Museum of Religious Art and a gift shop, as well as a shelter and soup kitchen for the homeless.
Amsterdam Ave/112th St.

St Mark's-in-the-Bowery

This church dates from 1799 and is built on the site of Peter Stuyvesant's farm (*see p48*). The Greek Revival steeple was added in 1826, and the cast-iron portico in 1858. Further restoration was carried out after the fire of 1978. The church is old in years, but young in outlook. Pews have been removed to allow dancers, poets, and performing artists to entertain.
East Village at 2nd Ave/10th St.

Trinity Church

In 1776, fire also destroyed the original building, chartered in 1697. The present much-visited building, in English Gothic style, was completed in 1846 and is the third on the site. It has a small museum.
Broadway, at the bottom of Wall St.

Church of the Ascension

Built in 1841, it was the first brownstone

Unpretentious St Paul's Chapel has had distinguished persons worship here

church and the first in English Gothic
Revival style. Special features are its
stained-glass windows by John La Farge
and its marble altar sculpture.
5th Ave/W 10th St.

Church of the Incarnation
Rich in stained glass, it is especially
noted for its Tiffany window in the
north aisle, depicting the 23rd Psalm,
and its two angel windows by William
Morris in the south aisle.
Madison Ave/35th St.

Church of Our Lady of Pompeii
This is where America's first saint, the
Italian immigrant Mother Cabrini, often
worshipped.
Bleecker St/6th Ave.

Church of the Transfiguration
This was the Zion Episcopal Church,
dating from 1801, long before the arrival
of the Chinese. Chinese Catholics now
worship here.
Mott St & Mosco St, Chinatown.

Church of the Transfiguration
Not to be confused with the Zion
Episcopal Church (above) and
associated with actors and writers, this
church has a La Farge window in the
south transept showing the legendary
19th-century actor Edwin Booth
playing Hamlet.
E 29th St.

Grace Church
An attractive 1846 Neo-Gothic building
where circus chief PT Barnum organised
midget Tom Thumb's wedding in 1863.
800 Broadway.

Trinity Church framed at one end of Wall Street

John Street United Methodist Church
On the site of America's first Methodist
church. Originating in 1768, it was
rebuilt in 1818 and 1841 and has a
brownstone façade.
44 John St.

St Paul's Chapel
New York's oldest public building in
continuous use dates from 1766. George
Washington worshipped here and his
pew is on view in the blue and pink
interior. The building is based on St
Martin-in-the-Fields, London.
Vesey St, Fulton St, & Broadway.

The Cloisters Museum

This branch of the Metropolitan Museum of Art overlooking the Hudson River specialises in medieval art and architecture. Colonnaded walks lead between French and Spanish cloisters, a 12th-century chapterhouse, a chapel, and other imported monastic buildings.
Fort Tryon Park. Tel: (212) 923 3700. Open: Mar–Oct, Tue–Sun 9.30am–5.30pm; Nov–Feb, Tue–Sun 9.30am–4.45pm. Subway: 190th St.

Con Edison Energy Museum

Here you can see the story of electricity, from Thomas Edison's inventions to the question of sources for the future, told through exhibitions and displays.
*145 E 14th St/3rd Ave.
Tel: (212) 460 6244.
Open: Tue–Sat 9am–5pm.
Free admission. Subway: 3rd Ave.*

Cooper-Hewitt Museum

Incorporating the Smithsonian Institution's National Museum of Design, this is the only museum in the USA devoted to contemporary and historical design. The collection covers textiles, jewellery, and other ornamental works, and architectural drawings.
*5th Ave/91st St. Tel: (212) 860 6868.
Open: Tue 10am–9pm, Wed–Sat 10am–5pm, Sun noon–5pm.
Admission charge (Tue free 5–9pm).
Subway: Lexington Ave/86th St.*

Diamond District

A block at West 47th Street, between Fifth and Sixth Avenues, comprises the wholesale jewellery trading district, dominated by bearded Orthodox Jews in black. Diamonds are cut and polished, jewellery repaired, set, and deals made above the ground-level shops.
Subway: 47th–50th sts/Rockefeller Center.

Dyckman House

Furnished in original 18th-century style, this is the only remaining Dutch farmhouse in Manhattan. It was presented to the city by the Dyckman family in 1915.
*204th St/Broadway. Tel: (212) 304 9422.
Open: Tue–Sun 11am–7pm.
Subway: 190th St.*

East Village

See Walk *pp48–9.*

El Museo del Barrio

The only museum in the United States exclusively devoted to the art and culture of Puerto Rico and Latin America. Founded in 1969 and based in Harlem, the museum provides a fascinating insight into the neighbourhood and its people.
*1230 5th Ave/104th St.
Tel: (212) 831 7272. Open: Wed–Sun 11am–5pm, Thu noon–7pm. Donation suggested.
Subway: Lexington Ave/103rd St.*

Ellis Island National Monument

Ellis Island *(see p50)* is one of 40 islands around New York. A museum traces the history of immigration to America. The Circle Line, Statue of Liberty ferry has daily departures from the South Ferry at Battery Park.
Tel: (212) 363 3200. Ferry departures: daily 9.30am–3.30pm. Free admission with ferry ticket. Subway: Bowling St.

Midtown and Uptown Manhattan

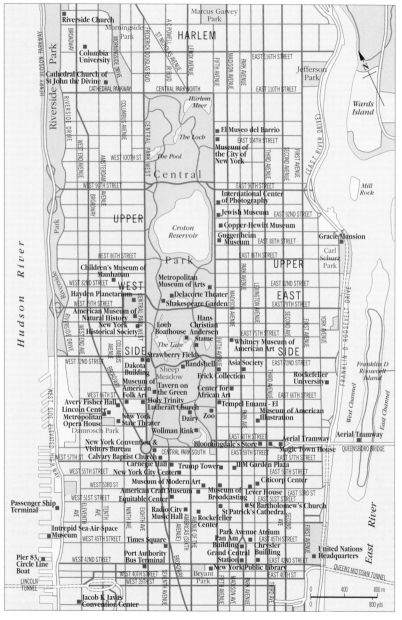

Marcus Garvey Park

HARLEM

Riverside Church
Morningside Park
Columbia University
Cathedral Church of St John the Divine
Jefferson Park
Wards Island
El Museo del Barrio
Museum of the City of New York
Mill Rock
International Center of Photography
Jewish Museum
Copper-Hewitt Museum
Guggenheim Museum
Gracie Mansion
Carl Schurz Park
Children's Museum of Manhattan
UPPER EAST SIDE
Metropolitan Museum of Arts
Delacorte Theater
Shakespeare Garden
Hayden Planetarium
American Museum of Natural History
New York Historical Society
Hans Christian Andersen Statue
Loeb Boathouse
Whitney Museum of American Art
Strawberry Fields
Dakota Building
Bandshell
Asia Society
Sheep Meadow
Frick Collection
Rockefeller University
Museum of American Folk Art
Tavern on the Green
Center for African Art
Franklin D Roosevelt Island
Avery Fisher Hall
Lincoln Center
Metropolitan Opera House
Holy Trinity Lutheran Church
New York State Theater
Dairy
Zoo
Tempel Emanu - El
Museum of American Illustration
Wollman Rink
New York Convention & Visitors Bureau
Bloomingdale's Store
Magic Town House
Aerial Tramway
Aerial Tramway
Calvary Baptist Church
Carnegie Hall
Trump Tower
IBM Garden Plaza
New York City Center
Museum of Modern Art
Citicorp Center
American Craft Museum
Equitable Center
Museum of Broadcasting
Lever House
St Bartholomew's Church
Passenger Ship Terminal
Radio City Music Hall
Rockefeller Center
St Patrick's Cathedral
Park Avenue Atrium
Intrepid Sea-Air-Space Museum
Pan Am Building
Chrysler Building
Pier 83, Circle Line Boat
Port Authority Bus Terminal
Times Square
Grand Central Station
United Nations Headquarters
New York Public Library
Bryant Park
LINCOLN TUNNEL
Jacob K Javits Convention Center

Hudson River

Riverside Park

Central Park

UPPER WEST SIDE

Croton Reservoir

The Lake

Harlem Meer

The Loch

The Pool

East River

QUEENSBORO BRIDGE

QUEENS MIDTOWN TUNNEL

0   400   800 m
0   800 yds

Walk: East Village

Highly fashionable in the 19th century, when it was the home of the wealthy, East Village later became a more workaday place for several decades. In the 1950s it attracted the beatniks. Now it has been regentrified.

Allow 1 hour.

Begin at the Astor Place subway station. Head east along Stuyvesant St.

1 Stuyvesant Street

The land surrounding this street was once part of the Dutch governor Peter Stuyvesant's farm or *bouwerie*, from which the nearby thoroughfare got its name. There are some fine 19th-century houses, including No. 21, built in 1804 as a wedding gift for his great-great granddaughter. At the end of the street is the Church of St Mark's-in-the-

Bowery, at the corner of Second Avenue and East 10th Street on the site of the mansion where Stuyvesant lived (*see p44*). The church opened in 1799, and since 1920 has been a centre for avant-garde cultural activity as well as worship.

Turn right along 2nd Ave.

2 Second Avenue

The street was a thriving ethnic theatre district in the early 1900s. Stars set into the sidewalk pay tribute to Yiddish performers of that time. Also see the Ukrainian Museum at No. 203.

Continue down 2nd Ave to St Mark's Place.

3 St Mark's Place

The East Village end of East 8th Street, St Mark's Place was the centre of the Beat Generation when Allen Ginsberg, Jack Kerouac, and other 1950s writers lived here.

An earlier resident – at No. 77 – was the British-born poet WH Auden. Between Second and Third avenues, St Mark's Place has offbeat stores, vegetarian restaurants, stalls and boutiques selling jewellery, leather goods, and clothing. At St Mark's Bookshop (No. 12) you can spend time

among the volumes, and find out about local events from the bulletin board.
Turn right into St Mark's Place and left on to 3rd Ave to E 7th St.

4 East 7th Street
At No. 15 is McSorley's Old Ale House, opened in 1854, and a haunt of Brendan Behan, the Irish dramatist. It is popular with students from local colleges. Nearby, the Ukrainian Shop and St George's Ukrainian Catholic Church reflect a thriving ethnic community.
Continue along 3rd Ave to Cooper Square.

5 Cooper Square
The square is dominated by the seven-storey brownstone Cooper Union Foundation Building, founded in 1859 by Peter Cooper as a non fee-paying college for working-class students, giving them the chance of an education he never had. His statue stands in the square. Public speakers were invited to use the Great Hall of the college of art, architecture, and engineering, among them Abraham Lincoln, who attacked slavery in an electioneering address.
Walk north along 4th Ave to the junction with St Mark's Place, turning left into Astor Place.

6 Astor Place
Two traffic islands on the junction are spectacularly ornamented. A cast-iron sculpture marks a subway entrance, and the vast rotating black cube, *Alamo*, is by Bernard Rosenthal. At No. 2 queues frequently form outside Astor Place Hair Design, where cheap and sometimes outrageous styling is offered.
Turn left into Lafayette St.

7 Lafayette Street
On the right, Colonnade Row has four houses dating from 1833, once occupied by the millionaires Astor and Vanderbilt. Across the road at No. 425 is the Shakespeare Festival's Public Theater, in Italian Renaissance style. It was originally opened by Astor in 1854 as New York's first free library. One of the earliest venues for Off-Broadway productions, the Public Theater – five playhouses and a cinema – was opened by Joseph Papp in the late 1960s with the rock musical, *Hair*. The theater has also been involved in a Shakespeare Marathon, with the object of performing each of the Bard's works over a six-year period.
Continue down Lafayette St, turning right into Bleecker St.

8 Bleecker Street
Number 65 is the 1898 Bayard Building, the only New York structure designed by the famous Chicago skyscraper architect, Louis Sullivan.
Return to Lafayette St for the Bleecker St subway station.

The Village has its own unique flavour

Ellis Island

Visitors to the Ellis Island Museum of Immigration (*see p46*), opened in 1990, will not find it difficult to visualise the scene when immigrants, mainly from Europe, arrived on American soil after long, crowded, and often arduous voyages. Many feared desperately that they would be turned back for health or other reasons. However, 17 million new Americans were 'processed' – each took about four hours – and were allowed entry between 1892 and 1954.

Close your eyes in the museum and you can imagine shuffling along in a seemingly never-ending line of weary hopefuls, pausing for medical checks, for the scrutinising of documents, and for questions, questions, questions in an alien tongue, voices reverberating off the thick walls. Most had reached their promised land, and would be admitted to form ethnic neighbourhoods in New York, or to put down roots elsewhere in the USA. Others, about 10 per cent, were unacceptable, and ordered to be despatched home. Some could not face this and quietly committed suicide – up to half a dozen a month, some 3,000 in all. Some of those who were rejected flung themselves from the deck of the ship carrying them homeward, hoping to swim across to Manhattan's shore, and perished in the attempt.

Even from the shore, Ellis Island evokes an atmosphere of foreboding, its dark brick buildings reminiscent of a 19th-century workhouse. But it also generates a strong sense of not-so-distant history. Two in five Americans won US citizenship via Ellis Island in the early days, and for them, as well as for overseas visitors today, the resurrected immigration station is a deeply thought-provoking experience.

Once filled with anxious immigrants, this stately building is now the Ellis Island Museum

Downtown Manhattan

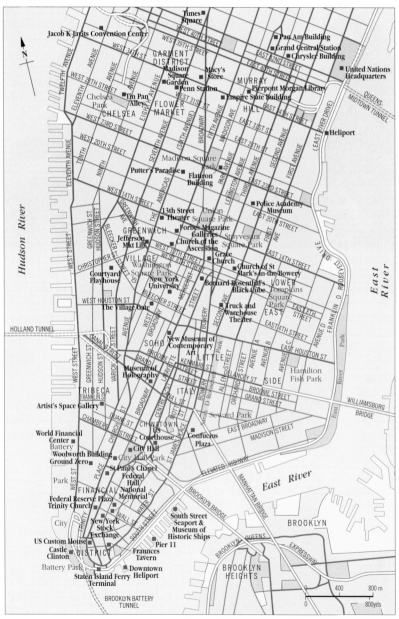

- Times Square
- Jacob K Javits Convention Center
- Pan Am Building
- Grand Central Station
- Chrysler Building
- GARMENT DISTRICT
- United Nations Headquarters
- Madison Square Garden
- Macy's Store
- MURRAY HILL
- Penn Station
- Pierpont Morgan Library
- Empire State Building
- Chelsea Park
- Tin Pan Alley
- CHELSEA
- FLOWER MARKET
- Madison Square Park
- Putter's Paradise
- Flatiron Building
- Police Academy Museum
- 13th Street Theater
- Union Square Park
- Forbes Magazine Galleries
- GREENWICH VILLAGE
- Jefferson Mkt Lib
- Church of the Ascension
- Stuyvesant Square Park
- Grace Church
- Church of St Mark's-in-the-Bowery
- Courtyard Playhouse
- Washington Square Park
- New York University
- Bernard Rosenthal's Black Cube
- LOWER EAST SIDE
- Tompkins Square Park
- The Village Gate
- Truck and Warehouse Theater
- EAST VILLAGE
- SOHO
- New Museum of Contemporary Art
- LITTLE ITALY
- Hamilton Fish Park
- Museum of Holography
- TRIBECA
- Artist's Space Gallery
- Seward Park
- CHINATOWN
- World Financial Center
- US Courthouse
- Confucius Plaza
- City Hall
- Battery
- Woolworth Building
- Ground Zero
- City Hall Park
- St Paul's Chapel
- Federal Hall
- National Memorial
- FINANCIAL DISTRICT
- Federal Reserve Plaza
- Trinity Church
- New York Stock Exchange
- South Street Seaport & Museum of Historic Ships
- US Custom House
- Castle Clinton
- Fraunces Tavern
- Pier 11
- Battery Park
- Downtown Heliport
- Staten Island Ferry Terminal
- BROOKLYN HEIGHTS

Hudson River

East River

East River

BROOKLYN

QUEENS

QUEENS-MIDTOWN TUNNEL

Heliport

FRANKLIN D ROOSEVELT DRIVE

WILLIAMSBURG BRIDGE

MANHATTAN BRIDGE

BROOKLYN BRIDGE

ELEVATED HIGHWAY

BROOKLYN-QUEENS EXPRESSWAY

HOLLAND TUNNEL

BROOKLYN BATTERY TUNNEL

0   400   800 m

0   800yds

The observatory on top of the Empire State Building

Empire State Building

This 102-storey, 1,454-foot Art Deco office block structure – the height includes a TV transmitter mast – opened in 1931. Observatories at the 86th and 102nd levels give views of parts of four states, and the 86th floor has an outdoor promenade. Changing exhibitions are held in the lobby at the Fifth Avenue entrance. Children will enjoy the animated King Kong display and Eight Wonders of the World exhibit. Skyride is a thrilling simulated trip around the landmarks of Manhattan.
34th St/5th Ave. Tel: (212) 736 3100.
Open: daily 9.30am–midnight (last elevator up at 11.30pm). Admission charge. Subway: 6th Ave/34th St.

Federal Hall National Memorial

A Doric temple-style building erected in 1842 on the site of Washington's inauguration as first president of the USA on 30 April 1789. It contains a museum of New York's Colonial and early Federal periods, with exhibits, films, and 18th-century folk music.
26 Wall St. Tel: (212) 825 6888.
Open: Mon–Fri 9am–5pm. Free admission. Subway: Broad St/Wall St.

Federal Reserve Bank of New York

A bank for banks, with more gold stored in its subterranean vaults than in Fort Knox. The imposing building is modelled on the Strozzi Palace in Florence. The wealth of nations is locked away in private chambers, shifting from nation to nation in a short move from one chamber to another.
33 Liberty St. Tel: (212) 720 6130.
One-hour guided tour by appointment with minimum five days' notice, Mon–Fri 10.30am, 11.30am, 1.30pm, & 2.30pm. Free admission. Subway: Wall St/William St.

Fraunces Tavern Museum

Five historic buildings, including the restored 18th-century tavern where, in the Long Room, Washington bade farewell to his officers celebrating the British leaving New York after the Revolutionary War in 1783. The restaurant has existed for more than 200 years. There is a bar room and a gift shop. The museum has decorative arts, paintings, prints, manuscripts, period rooms, 18th- and 19th-century memorabilia – including Washington's teeth and hair – and changing exhibitions. Lectures, concerts, and other events are staged.
54 Pearl St/Broad St. Tel: (212) 425 1778. Open: Mon–Fri 10am–4.45pm, Sat noon–4pm. Admission charge. Subway: Whitehall St/South Ferry.

Forbes Magazine Galleries

Permanent exhibition of the late publisher Malcolm Forbes's collection of 500 toy boats, 12,000 toy soldiers, and the world's largest clutch of Fabergé eggs. Trophies and documents are displayed, and there are changing exhibitions of paintings.
62 5th Ave. Tel: (212) 206 5548. Open: Tue, Wed, Fri, & Sat 10am–4pm. Free admission. Subway: Union Square.

Frick Collection

More like a home than most major galleries, this 1935 Beaux Arts mansion is much as it was when industrialist Henry C Frick lived here, with a fortune in European Old Masters from the 14th to 19th centuries. When the feet are tired, relax among the fountains and greenery in the glass-ceilinged courtyard.

1 E 70th St. Tel: (212) 288 0700. Open: Tue–Sat 10am–6pm, Sun 1–6pm. Audio-visual shows: 10.30am–4.30pm at hourly intervals. Admission charge. Subway: Lexington Ave/68th St.

Gracie Mansion (1799)

Federal-style frame house in Carl Schurz Park that has been the official residence of New York's mayors since 1942 (*see p96*). Period items loaned from private collections are displayed, and there is a permanent 'Merchants to Mayors' exhibition in the basement.
East End Ave at 89th St. Tel: (212) 570 4751. Open: end Mar–mid-Nov. Tours on Wed by appointment only. Children and students free. Subway: Lexington Ave/86th St.

Grand Central Station

See p60.

The Federal Hall National Memorial Building

Greenwich Village

Oddly enough, Greenwich Village does not have much in the way of formal sights – museums, churches, and the like – but the character of its streets varies from the picturesque to the eccentric. The best thing is to wander, look, and flop on to a bar stool or café chair now and then to reflect on what you have seen. There will have been plenty in this engaging and stimulating community.

Café society is part of the Village lifestyle

Bedford Street

One of the quietest and most desirable of Village streets. Among its quaint houses is No. 751/2, just over nine feet wide, and New York's narrowest dwelling. The clapboard house next door was built in 1799 and is said to be the oldest in the Village. At No. 80 is Chumleys, a speakeasy during the prohibition days, but now a cosy bar and restaurant. James Joyce finished writing *Ulysses* at one of its tables.
Subway: Christopher St/Sheridan Square.
Bus: M13.

Bleecker Street, Sixth Avenue

The lively heart of Greenwich Village. The area around the intersection has lots of shops, bars, and sidewalk cafés, and is a meeting place for New York University students and others in the young set. The Café Figaro and others nearby were where the Beat writers got together in the 1950s (*see p58*).
Subway: Christopher St/Sheridan Square.
Bus: M5 & M6.

Christopher Street

Running from West Street, fronting the Hudson River, to Sheridan Square, the street is the focal point for the Village's gay community.
Subway: Christopher St/Sheridan Square.
Bus: M13.

Church of the Ascension

A small, Gothic-style brownstone church designed by Richard Upjohn, architect of Trinity Church in the Financial District. It has a La Farge altarpiece and some fine stained-glass windows.
Northwest corner of 5th Ave & W 10th St.
Subway: Broadway/W 8th St.
Bus: M2, M3, & M5.

Grey Art Gallery

Part of the art department of New York University, with a permanent collection of post-1940s American works.

In addition, contemporary art is featured in the many changing exhibitions held here.
33 Washington Place. East side of Washington Square. Tel: (212) 998 6780. Open: Sep–May, Tue, Thu, & Fri 11am–6.30pm, Wed 11am–8.30pm, Sat 11am–5pm; Jun–Aug, weekdays 11am–7pm. Donation suggested.
Subway: Broadway/W 8th St.
Bus: M2, M3, & M13.

Jefferson Market Courthouse

Built as a courthouse in 1876, the building is now used as a branch of the New York Public Library. Because of its alternating bands of red brick and granite, locals describe the building as being in the Lean Bacon style of architecture. It is, in fact, Victorian Gothic, and one of its architects was Calvert Vaux, of Central Park fame.
425 6th Ave. Subway: Christopher St/Sheridan Square. Bus: M5 & M6.

The Lion's Head

Literary bar with clients' book jackets pasted on the walls; a favourite watering hole for *Village Voice* journalists.
59 Christopher St, opposite Christopher Park with statue of Civil War General Philip Sheridan. Subway: Christopher St/Sheridan Square. Bus: M13.

Patchin Place

A courtyard of neat mews cottages which has been home at various times to such literary figures as John Masefield, Theodore Dreiser, Eugene O'Neill, and e e cummings.
W 10th St, just west of 6th Ave. Subway: Christopher St/Sheridan Square. Bus: M5 & M6.

Washington Square

Chess players, rollerskaters, street entertainers, art shows – hardly the Washington Square novelist Henry James wrote about in his novel of that name, but still the nominal centre of Greenwich Village. It is dominated by the triumphal arch commemorating the centenary of George Washington's inauguration as president. Most of the surrounding buildings belong to New York University.
Subway: W 10th St/Washington Square. Bus: M5 & M6.

The White Horse Tavern

An inexpensive bar with literary connections dating to the late 1880s. This is the one in which Welsh poet Dylan Thomas, author of *Under Milk Wood* and a prodigious drinker, drank his last. Academics still gather here, especially in the outdoor café open in warm weather.
567 Hudson St. Tel: (212) 243 9260. Subway: Christopher St/Sheridan Square. Bus: M10.

Washington Square was the setting for Henry James's novel of love and betrayal

Walk: Greenwich Village

Greenwich Village manages to retain a hint of a rural atmosphere – there were still farms here in the 19th century. Some of its winding streets are former cattle trails and country lanes.

Allow 2 hours.

Begin at Washington Square at the south end of 5th Ave (subway station at West 4th St/Washington Square). Proceed clockwise round the square.

1 Washington Square

Washington Arch was first built in wood, and later, in 1895, in stone by Stanford White to commemorate the centenary of the inauguration of the first US president. Most buildings around the square are part of New York University. The oldest, 20 Washington Square North, dates from before 1830.

The Grey Gallery, in the university's main building, exhibits mainly contemporary art. The Loeb Students' Center stands on the site of The House of Genius, which has housed writers such as Theodore Dreiser, O Henry, and Eugene O'Neill.

At the square's southwest corner, turn left into MacDougal St.

2 MacDougal Street

Numbers 130 and 132 were the home of Louisa M Alcott, who wrote *Little Women* there. The nearby Provincetown

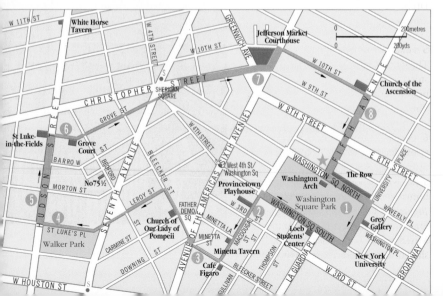

Playhouse staged premiere performances of Eugene O'Neill's plays.
Continue along MacDougal St to Bleecker St.

3 Bleecker Street

Although home of the Village's Italian community, Bleecker Street is a cosmopolitan thoroughfare. Its junction with MacDougal Street and Sixth Avenue has sidewalk cafés popularised by literary figures in the 1950s. On the opposite side of Sixth Avenue is the Church of Our Lady of Pompeii, where the first American saint, Italian-born Mother Cabrini, worshipped (*see p45*).
Cross 6th Ave. Continue along Bleecker St, turning left into Leroy St. Cross 7th Ave to enter St Luke's Place.

4 St Luke's Place

This row of elegant mid-19th-century brownstone houses includes the house (No. 16) in which novelist Theodore Dreiser wrote *An American Tragedy*.
Turn right into Hudson St.

5 Hudson Street

The Church of St Luke-in-the-Fields stood by the river bank when it was built in 1821.
Turn right down Grove St.

6 Grove Street

Grove Street and parallel Christopher Street form New York's best-known gay area. Marie's Crisis Café was the former home of Thomas Paine, author of *The Rights of Man*. An iron gate on Grove Street marks Grove Court, once called Mixed Ale Alley because its impoverished residents pooled their beer.

Cross Sheridan Square into Christopher St and continue to 6th Ave.

7 Avenue of the Americas (Sixth Avenue)

In the triangle formed by Sixth Avenue, Greenwich Avenue, and West 10th Street, is located the former Jefferson Market Courthouse. It dates from 1876.
Cross 6th Ave and take W 10th St to 5th Ave.

8 Fifth Avenue

On the corner of West 10th Street and Fifth Avenue, the 1840 Church of the Ascension has stained-glass windows, and an altar mural by John La Farge.
Turn right on to 5th Ave and return to Washington Arch.

Washington Arch at the start of the Greenwich Village walk

The concept of 'village' life in a place as urban and urbane as New York may seem curious, if not downright pretentious. But two parts of the city not only carry the word 'village' as part of their name, but are also totally different from the rest in tempo and character.

Greenwich Village, which some residents of Manhattan dismiss these days as *passé*, continues to be what it has always been: a community apart. Although there is no longer a recognisable literati, there is an air of successful creativity among its elegant homes and quaint streets. Would-be writers gather at the Figaro and other sidewalk cafés, poring over the pages of *Village Voice* and putting the world to rights, though the attitudes they strike are less iconoclastic than those of the hell-raising Beat Generation writers who preceded them in the 1950s. Gay bars on Christopher Street, and events like Halloween, when strangely costumed crowds parade uninhibitedly through the streets, prove that Greenwich Village still attracts the unconventional and bohemian, if not the downright eccentric.

So does neighbouring East Village, on the other side of Broadway, where 8th Street becomes St Mark's Place, a bizarre bazaar of alternative-living stalls, stores, and restaurants. The area has always attracted offbeat writers and artists and revolutionary thinkers. This was where Edward Albee (*Who's Afraid of Virginia Woolf*), Theodore Dreiser, and e e cummings lived, where the author of *Moby Dick*, Herman Melville, worked as a customs inspector when he was unable to earn his living as a writer, and where he began *Billy Budd*, his last novel. George Gershwin gave his first public recital here, and the Astors and Vanderbilts initially lived here. This was where Jack Kerouac, Allen Ginsberg, and other Beat Generation figures lived it up; avant-garde theatre thrives here yet. Gentrification is putting a new shine on East Village, but it, too, will always be just that little bit different.

Facing page above: charming house fronts in Washington Square; below: villagers out for a stroll. Above: Bleecker Street is at the heart of the Village

Grand Central Station

Not just a railway terminal, more an art form, and certainly a great engineering feat. Built in the Renaissance style over a 10-year period, it opened in 1913 with a vast main concourse – one of the world's largest rooms. It is 470 feet long, and the barrel-vaulted ceiling, with 2,500 stars painted on a night sky background, is 150 feet high. There are huge windows, and sculptures of Mercury, Athena, and Hercules decorate the station clock. Elevated Park Avenue runs over the top of the Grand Central, which was declared a national landmark in 1978, thwarting a proposal to put up an office block at the site. Railway tracks at two levels carry more than 550 trains daily. The recently renovated dining concourse at the tower level includes the Oyster Bar, and offers a wide selection of cuisine. Free tours of the station are held at 12.30pm on Wednesdays.
42nd St/Lexington Ave.
Tel: (212) 532 4900.
Subway: Grand Central Station.

Grant's Tomb

Near Columbia University, this is the granite mausoleum where Civil War General Ulysses S Grant, twice US President, and his wife are buried. The tomb is a national monument, with photographs and memorabilia.
Riverside Drive/122nd St.
Tel: (212) 666 1640/1668.
Open: daily 9am–5pm.
Subway: Broadway/125th St.

Magnificent architecture of the Grand Central Station, with the Chrysler Building in the background

Guggenheim Museum

Modern art sometimes raises eyebrows, and when the museum opened in 1959 Frank Lloyd Wright's setting for it certainly did. The museum displays some of the priceless works which 19th-century multimillionaire Solomon Guggenheim collected from Europe, as well as some rare photographs of his contemporaries. Themed, and other temporary exhibitions of the work of 20th-century artists are held from time to time.

5th Ave/E 89th St. Tel: (212) 423 3500. Open: Sun–Wed 9am–6pm, Fri & Sat 9am–8pm. Closed: Thu. Admission charge (free Tue 5–7.45pm). Subway: Lexington Ave/86th St.

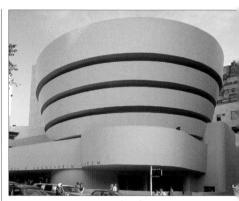

Inside and outside, the Guggenheim Museum is a fascinating structure

International Center of Photography

Photography is very much the American art form. Here there are exhibitions of photographs from the 19th century to the present day, representing most of the world's leading practitioners, and also temporary shows of innovative work, some of it by local photographers.

5th Ave/94th St. Tel: (212) 860 1777. Open: Tue–Thu 10am–5pm, Fri 10am–8pm, Sat & Sun 10am–6pm. Admission charge. Subway: Lexington Ave/96th St. Also on 1133 Ave of the Americas/43rd St. Tel: (212) 860 1777.

Intrepid Sea-Air-Space Museum

This famous World War II aircraft carrier is now a museum depicting events and armed conflicts around the world, up to and including the Gulf War, and the science and technology of the planes and ships involved. The world's fastest aircraft, spy-in-the-sky,

and guided missile submarines are all represented here.

Pier 86, foot of W 46th St at Hudson River. Tel: (212) 245 0072. Open: Mon–Fri 10am–5pm, Sat & Sun 10am–7pm. Admission charge. Subway: Fulton St/William St.

Jewish Museum

This is America's most significant institution devoted to Jewish history and culture. The museum holds the largest collection of Jewish ceremonial objects in the western hemisphere, many of which were rescued from European synagogues before World War II. Also displayed here are historical exhibits, art works, and manuscripts. Exhibits demonstrate the poverty of Lower East Side immigrants, and the Holocaust sufferings.

5th Ave/92nd St. Tel: (212) 423 3200. Open: Mon, Wed, Thu, & Sun 11am–5.45pm, Tue 11am–8pm, Sun 11am–6pm. Admission charge. Subway: Lexington Ave/96th St.

Harlem

The scene of civil rights riots during the 1960s, and still associated in many minds with urban dereliction, Harlem is undergoing restoration. It remains a mecca for black culture. You can reach it by bus or the subway, though at night it would be wiser to take a taxi. Bus and walking tours are available (*see p185*). Some Harlem streets have been renamed out of respect for the area's black heritage, such as Lenox Avenue, now Malcolm X Boulevard. The area is famous for its nightlife – pick up a copy of *Harlem's Culture: Guide to Great Events.*

Harlem is the heart of black New York

Abyssinian Baptist Church

Built in Gothic style, this bluestone building is noted less for its architecture than for its former incumbent, the Revd Adam Clayton Powell Jr, America's first black Congressman, and for its lively Sunday services with a belt-it-out choir and fire-and-brimstone sermons.
131 W 138th St. Tel: (212) 368 4471. Sunday services: 11am.

Apollo Theater

Opened in 1913 as a music hall for whites only, the Apollo's stage was ultimately graced by such artistes as Ella Fitzgerald, Billie Holiday, Aretha Franklin, Count Basie, and Duke Ellington. After being closed for a time in the 1970s, it was restored and opened again in 1986. It has lively amateur performances on Wednesday nights.
253 W 125th St. Tel: (212) 749 5838.

Black Fashion Museum

Costumes used in black film, theatre, and television productions are displayed. More than 5,000 exhibits from the distant past to the contemporary, including children's clothes, reflect the importance of the growth and development of the fashion industry to the African-American community, with black designers' flair for colour and style.
155 W 126th St. Tel: (212) 666 1320. Open: weekdays noon–8pm. Visitors welcome. Donation suggested.

Canaan Baptist Church of Christ

Gospel music at its best, performed during Sunday services.
132 W 116th St. Sunday services: 10.45am. Subway: W 116th St (Malcolm X Blvd, or 8th Ave).

Malcolm Shabazz Mosque

Topped by an aluminium dome, this former casino has been a place of worship for black Muslims since the 1960s. Malcolm X used to preach here.
102 W 116th St. Subway: 116th St/Malcolm X Blvd.

Marcus Garvey Park

A rocky area cutting across Fifth Avenue between 120th and 124th streets, the park honours a black leader who headed a back-to-Africa movement between the two World Wars. It is surrounded by many splendid late 19th-century houses in the Mount Morris Historic District.
Subway: W or E 116th St.

Schomburg Center for Research in Black Culture

More than 100,000 books, photographs, and documents collected by Arthur Schomburg, a Puerto Rican immigrant (1940) are on display. The American Negro Theater is a recent addition.
515 Malcolm X Blvd. Tel: (212) 491 2200. Open: Mon–Wed noon–8pm, Thu noon–6pm, Fri–Sat 10am–6pm, Sun 1–5pm. Free admission.
Subway: 135th St/Malcolm X Blvd.

Strivers' Row

These two rows were built in the 1890s to show that attractive dwellings could be built cheaply, and since the end of World War I they have been occupied by black middle-class professionals who from the start were seen by their less fortunate neighbours as strivers after the good life.
W 138th & W 139th sts between 7th & 8th aves.

Studio Museum

A small art museum housing a large collection of paintings, sculptures, and photographs. The museum has changing exhibitions and a programme of lectures. There is also a gift shop.
W 124th St. Tel: (212) 864 4500. Open: Wed & Thu noon–6pm, Fri, noon–8pm, Sat & Sun 10am–6pm. Admission charge.

Organised walking tours take in the key sights of Harlem

Starting with Christopher Columbus who brought the first blacks to America in 1492, millions of black Africans came to the New World as slaves over the next

four centuries. By the early 1700s, New York had become the trading centre for slaves to be sent on to Latin America and the Caribbean regions to work on sugar, coffee, and cotton plantations. Though slavery was not initially a major part of New York's economy, it had become big business by the 1730s. African New Yorkers worked as house servants, they cleared forests, built roads, and helped on farms. During English rule, a considerable number became skilled artisans, blacksmiths, coopers, and carpenters, working on contract for their owners. Later, European immigration scattered the African American population to isolated pockets in the city.

In 1940, 94 per cent of the population of New York was white.By 1980, the proportion had dropped to 61 per cent. The movement of black people into the city, which had started with runaway slaves from the South even before the Civil War, accelerated during the 1920s, and continued even faster after World War II when Puerto Ricans also started to arrive. Caribbean

immigration became prevalent in the 1960s. By 1980, the black population had reached just over one and three quarter million – about one in four of the city's total – a further one and a quarter million of the population were Hispanic, 852,000 of them Puerto Ricans.

Facing page above: the black community is an integral part of city life; below: an African art street stall
Above: the tradition of gospel singing has enriched American faith and music; left: basketball stars in the making in Central Park

Lincoln Center for the Performing Arts

Six separate concert halls and theatres seating a total of 18,000, built in the 1960s, cover eight blocks. The centre is home to the New York Philharmonic, the Metropolitan Opera Company, and the New York City Opera and Ballet.
Broadway/64th St. Tel: (212) 875 5350. Admission charge for daily tours. Subway: Broadway/Lincoln Center.

Lower East Side Tenement Museum

America's first urban living history museum, interpreting the history of the immigrant. Allows only guided tours. Historic walking tours are offered in the discount shopping district; also dramatisations and exhibitions.
97 Orchard St, between Delancy & Broome sts. Tel: (212) 431 0233; www.tenement.org Guided tours: Tue–Fri every half hour from 1–4pm, Sat & Sun 11am–4.30pm. Admission charge. Subway: Delancy St/Essex St.

Madame Tussaud's New York

A $50 million attraction where you can spot nearly 200 celebrities.
42nd St between 7th & 8th aves. Tel: (212) 921 0768.

Madison Square Garden Center

The world-famous sports and entertainment centre seats 20,000. It is also used as a convention centre and office complex, and is host to the New York Knicks (basketball) and New York Rangers (ice hockey).
4 Penn Plaza, near 33rd St. Tel: (212) 465 6225; www.thegarden.com Subway: Penn Station.

Metropolitan Museum of Art

See pp 68–9.

Metropolitan Opera House and Backstage Tour

A 90-minute tour of scenery and costume shops, stage areas, and rehearsal facilities gives a captivating insight into the working of the Opera House. Reservations required, call weekdays.
Lincoln Center. Tel: (212) 582 3512; www.operaed.org Tours: weekdays 3.45pm, Sat 10am. Admission charge. Subway: Broadway/Lincoln Center.

Mormon Visitors' Center

Film shows on the origin of the church in New York State, and on ancient America, explain the beliefs of the Church of Jesus Christ of the Latter-Day Saints. There is also a Genealogy library for ancestor-tracing.
125 Columbus Ave. Tel: (212) 873 1690. Open: Tue 1–9pm, Wed–Fri 1–7pm, Sat 11am–5pm. Closed: Mon & Sun. Free admission. Subway: Broadway/Lincoln Center.

Morris-Jumel Mansion

Built in 1765 by Colonel and Mrs Roger Morris as a country home, this mansion was used briefly in 1776 as George Washington's headquarters. Non-historians may find more of interest in the love life of a later resident, Mrs Eliza Jumel.
65 Roger Morris Park, Jumel Terrace, 160th St/St Nicholas Ave. Tel: (212) 923 8008. Open: Wed–Sun 10am–4pm. Admission charge. Subway: St Nicholas Ave/163rd St.

Museum for African Art

Exhibitions change bi-annually, shown in two town houses. Displays of sculpture and other art forms, historic and contemporary. It also has a bookshop.
54 E 68th St. Tel: (212) 861 1200.
Open: Tue–Fri 2–5pm, Sun noon–5pm.
Public tours: Sun 2pm.
Donation suggested.
Subway: 68th St.

Museum of the American Indian

Devoted to the cultures of the North, Central, and South American Indian. This is the largest collection of Indian artefacts in the USA, and includes possessions of Sitting Bull and Geronimo, and some scalps.
1 Bowling Green, State & Whitehall sts.
Tel: (212) 514 3700; www.nmai.so.edu
Open: Fri–Wed 10am–5pm, Thu 10am–8pm. Museum shop open: 10am–4.45pm.
Free admission. Subway: Bowling Green.

Museum of the City of New York

Presents the city's development from a Dutch trading post to today's bustling metropolis. Exhibitions of furniture, art works, toys, dolls' houses, and costumes.
5th Ave/103rd St. Tel: (212) 534 1672;
www.mcny.org
Open: Wed–Sat 10am–5pm, Sun noon–5pm. Donation suggested.
Subway: Lexington Ave/103rd St.

Museum of American Folk Art

A 30,000 square-foot exhibition space showcasing America's folk heritage – paintings, furniture, pottery, and quilts.
2 Lincoln Square, Columbus Ave/66th St.
Tel: (212) 977 7170/595 9533.

Museum of Holography

Science and art combine with an exhibition on this three-dimensional photographic technique using laser beams, housed in a SoHo cast-iron building.
11 Mercer St, Grand & Canal sts.
Tel: (212) 925 0581.
Open: Tue–Sun 11am–6pm.
Subway: Canal St.

Museum of Modern Art

Housed on six floors, the museum has one of the world's foremost collections of art from 1880 to the present day. Outside there is a refreshing sculpture garden with trees and pools. The museum is undergoing extensive expansion to double its exhibition space.
11 W 53rd St. Tel: (212) 708 9400.
Open: daily 10.30am–6pm, Fri 10.30am–8.30pm. Closed: Wed.
Admission charge (on Fri, pay what you wish, 4.30–8.15pm).
Subway: 5th Ave/53rd St.

In front of Madison Square Garden Center

Metropolitan Museum of Art

To do justice to the Metropolitan Museum of Art, time is needed. Since only a limited amount of culture can be absorbed in, say, three or four hours, what you really need is to devote several half days to the Met until you have sated your particular appetite, at least until you are next in New York. The Met is a vast treasure house, occupying four blocks, and containing more than three million priceless exhibits.

A graceful stone statue at the Met

Self-discipline is required to get the best out of each visit. Study a plan of the three floors before you launch yourself out of the magnificent Great Hall, and decide which of your interests you want to indulge on each occasion. For instance, if 20th-century art is your forte, you will note that it is exhibited in the same position on each floor.

The museum is closed on Mondays. From Tuesday to Friday, free tours of the highlights of the museum leave the Great Hall about every 25 minutes, less often at weekends.

Inevitably, as happens with such a huge collection, not all sections are permanently open, so anyone planning a visit with one vital interest in mind would be advised to inquire in advance whether it is currently on display.

Because of the time it takes to deposit and retrieve outer wear, most people carry their overcoats around with them in winter, or even wear them in the well-heated galleries. If it is practical, dress lightly and, of course, wear your most comfortable shoes.

The Met is one of several museums which has a suggested contribution instead of a fixed admission charge. That contribution also allows admission on the same day to The Cloisters, a hilltop 'folly' way up north in Tryon Park, overlooking the Hudson River. It contains the Met's medieval collection. In summer, an hourly shuttle bus runs between the two.

The museum houses works of art from ancient civilisations to the present day. Among them are hundreds of world-famous masterpieces. As well as galleries of painting and sculpture, the museum has displays of tapestries, musical instruments, costumes, and ornaments.

The five major collections are European Painting, American Painting, Primitive Art, Medieval Painting, and Egyptian Antiquities. A hall on the ground floor recreates the Temple of Dendera (15 BC), built by the Roman emporer Augustus. The Primitive Art collection is in one of four new wings, the Michael C Rockefeller Wing, a memorial to Nelson Rockefeller's son, who disappeared in New Guinea more than 35 years ago. Splendidly ornamental armour, heraldic banners, and the finest collections of Japanese arms and armour outside Japan, are exhibited in the Arms and Armor Galleries.

The American Wing includes rooms dedicated to various periods in the nation's history. One of them is by Frank Lloyd Wright, designer of that controversial modern building, the Guggenheim Museum.

The Twentieth Century Art Collection has some riveting works from Europe and America in the Lila Acheson Wallis Wing. Above it, on the roof, open in the summer, is a garden of contemporary sculpture.

The design of the museum includes courtyard gardens with soaring glass roofs and delightfully restful green areas with interesting statuary. Tiffany glass can be seen along the balcony by the American Wing garden.

Also welcome are the unexpected glimpses of Central Park from various angles, that appear like living canvasses of landscapes and people.

The final pleasure is seeking a memento, or an art book from the museum shops.

1000 5th Ave at 82nd St. Tel: (212) 535 7710; www.metmuseum.org
Open: Tue–Thu & Sun 9.30am–5.15pm, Fri & Sat 9.30am–8.45pm.
Closed: Mon, Thanksgiving, Christmas Day, New Year's Day.
Subway: 86th St/Lexington Ave.

Special exhibitions at the Met are a regular feature of the New York cultural scene

New Museum of Contemporary Art

Devoted solely to the art and ideas of our time, this museum explores offbeat issues, and features changing exhibitions of international artists' work.
583 Broadway at Houston/Prince sts.
Tel: (212) 219 1222;
www.newmuseum.org Open: Wed & Sun
noon–6pm, Thu, Fri, & Sat noon–8pm.
Donation suggested. Subway: Prince St.

New York City Fire Museum

Collections of the city Fire Department and Home Insurance Company. A history of fire-fighting in the city.
278 Spring St. Tel: (212) 477 9523;
www.nyfiremuseum.org
Open: Tue–Sun 10am–4pm. Donation
suggested. Subway: Spring St.

New York Historical Society

American art and antiques, advertising art, original Audubon watercolours of birds and other wildlife, Tiffany lamps, and antique toys. Also, more than 4 million manuscripts, prints, and rare books.
170 Central Park West/77th St.
Tel: (212) 873 3400; www.nyhistory.org
Open: Tue–Sat 11am–5pm. Admission
charge. Subway: 79th St.

New York Public Library

Free one-hour tours and changing exhibitions are held in this marble-fronted landmark Beaux Arts building where New Yorkers congregate on the steps on fine days to eat their packed lunches. The book collection is one of the world's five largest – more than 6 million volumes in the research section alone. The Reading Room is where

Trotsky studied before the 1917 Russian Revolution.
5th Ave/42nd St. Tel: (212) 930 0800.
Open: Mon, Thu–Sat 10am–6pm, Tue &
Wed 11am–7.30pm. Closed: Sun.
Subway: 42nd St/Grand Central Station.

New York Stock Exchange

The visitors' gallery overlooks the trading hall, and the ceaseless activity is described by automatic narration in Japanese, German, French, Italian, and Spanish. There is also a gift shop.
Broad St at Wall St.
Tel: (212) 656 3000; www.nyse.com
Open: weekdays 9.20am–3.30pm.
Free tickets issued from Broad St entrance
(No. 20) from 9.05am.
Subway: Broad St/Wall St.

Pierpont Morgan Library

Collections of rare books, Old Masters' drawings (including Rembrandt), and manuscripts in an Italian palazzo-style house built in 1917. Among permanent displays are financier Pierpont Morgan's private study, the Gutenberg Bible, medieval ornaments in gold and enamel, and Renaissance painting and sculpture. Garden court.
29 E 36th St. Tel: (212) 685 0008.
Open: Tue–Thu 10.30am–5pm,
Fri 10.30am–8pm, Sat 10.30am–6pm,
Sun noon–6pm. Closed: Mon & holidays.
Subway: 33rd St/Park Ave.

Police Academy Museum

Night sticks and old uniforms in a huge collection of memorabilia of the NYPD.
235 E 20th St. Tel: (212) 477 9753.
Open: Mon–Fri 9am–3pm. Free
admission. Subway: 23rd St/Park Ave.

Radio City Music Hall

This 1930s Art Deco landmark building, within the Rockefeller Center, claims a list of superlatives: world's biggest indoor theatre for rock concerts and revues; world's biggest chandelier over the staircase; world's largest contour curtain – it weighs about three tonnes – and a mighty Wurlitzer. It is also home to the Rockettes dance troupe. Backstage tours are conducted on most days.

1260 Ave of the Americas/50th St.
Tel: (212) 307 7171; www.radiocity.com
Admission charge. Subway: Rockefeller Center.

Riverside Church

A 1930s inter-denominational church with a carillon of 74 bells – the world's largest – in its 356-foot tower. A small charge is made to take the elevator 20 storeys up to see the view. A socially and politically aware church, Riverside opens its doors to a range of community events and music, dance and drama.

490 Riverside Drive at 120th/122nd sts.
Tel: (212) 870 6700.
Tower open: Tue–Sat 11am–4pm, Sun 12.30–4pm. Closed: Mon.
Subway: Broadway/116th St.

Rockefeller Center

See pp72–3.

SoHo

See pp74–5.

St Patrick's Cathedral

Seat of the Archdiocese of New York. The building of this Gothic-style structure, by James Renwick, began in 1858 and was completed in 1874.

5th Ave/50th St.
Open: daily 8am–8.30pm.
Subway: Rockefeller Center.

St Patrick's Cathedral is the centre of Roman Catholic worship in New York

Rockefeller Center

Thinking big came naturally to financier John D Rockefeller Jr. In the late 1920s, in defiance of the thick cloud of depression hanging low over North America and the West, he decided to go ahead with a long-held ambition: to create an architectural business and entertainment complex in the centre of Manhattan.

Atlas supporting the world

The Rockefeller Center is a 19-building, 22-acre complex providing a base for much of the nation's television programming, and headquarters for international corporations.

Underground concourses with shops and restaurants link the buildings. The Lower Plaza, where the 159 flags of the United Nations fly, was created as a focal point. A promenade between the Plaza and Fifth Avenue is lined with beds of flowers, changing with the seasons, but always providing colour.

From October to April the Plaza features a skating rink. In the warm months it becomes the Summer Garden Restaurant, presided over by an 18-foot bronze figure of Prometheus, covered with gold leaf – arguably the city's most photographed statue.

The flagship of the Center is the 70-storey Rockefeller Plaza skyscraper, and the boundaries of the complex extend from 47th Street to 51st Street, and between Fifth and Sixth avenues.

On the entertainments side, the Radio City Music Hall (*see p71 & p149*), with world-class performers on the stage, is based at the Center. Among a number of NBC-TV network programmes transmitted from studios in the complex is the early-morning *Today* show, tuned into by millions around the world.

John D Rockefeller Senior (the D is for Davison), whose fortune came from the Standard Oil Company which he founded, was born in 1839, and was an old man when his plans for the Center were formulated.

One aspect of his dream, however, never became reality. He had dearly wanted to support a civic drive to provide a new home for the Metropolitan Opera within the Center. The harsh economic climate of the times, leading to the 1929 Wall Street Crash, forced him to put aside that project. However, even without it, the developers of the Rockefeller Center achieved what they set out to do – to construct a city-within-a-city, making optimum use of air, light, and transportation facilities.

Up-market shops selling a wide range of goods surround the Lower Plaza, and are also at ground level of most of the Center's skyscrapers. Theatres and a variety of restaurants are dotted about. Probably the most famous restaurant is the Rainbow Room, at 30 Rockefeller Plaza. It is at the top of the GE Building (formerly the RCA Building until

General Electric took it over a few years ago), and has panoramic views of the Manhattan skyline. This is the place to go for ballroom dancing and 1930s-style glamour. At the same premises are the Rainbow Promenade, with pre- and after-theatre menus, and the Rainbow and Stars cabaret-supper club, open until 2am on weekdays.

American regional specialities can be enjoyed at the American Festival Café overlooking the Ice Rink or Summer Garden, depending on the season. It is not difficult to spend an entire day at the Center. Early birds can try the Japanese breakfast served from 6am at Café New York in the New York Hilton and Towers at concourse level.
47th–52nd sts west of 5th Ave.
Tel: (212) 632 4000.
Information at 30 Rockefeller Plaza (concourse level); call for opening hours.
Subway: Rockefeller Center.

A pleasant place to pass a day

The sumptuous statue of Prometheus dominates the Rockefeller Plaza

Walk: SoHo

Barely 30 years ago, SoHo (SOuth of HOuston Street) was described as a commercial slum, and there was a strong move to tear the place down. It was saved by preservationists and a powerful artistic lobby.

Allow 1 hour.

Begin at Broadway/Lafayette subway station. Head south on Broadway.

1   Broadway

At No. 583, on the west sidewalk, is the New Museum of Contemporary Art, the key word being 'new', because no exhibit is more than 10 years old. Much of the work is by as yet unrecognised experimental artists. Other art galleries are nearby. Just beyond Prince Street is the 1904 'Little' Singer Building, whose cast-iron construction and innovative wide windows set the style for the architecture of the 1950s. Food, presented as an art form, can be seen at the up-market Dean and DeLuca store across the street. At the northeast corner of Broome Street and Broadway is the building that has been called the cast-iron palazzo – the Haughwout, built in 1857 to a design inspired by the architecture of Venice.

Turn right into Broome St, then left into Mercer St.

2   Mercer Street

Evidence of the street's resident industry can be found in the fabric remnants thrown out from upstairs garment workshops. At No. 85 is Enchanted Forest, an intriguing shop stocked with children's crafts, books, and hand-made toys in a sylvan setting. At No. 11 is the Museum of Holography where pictures developed by laser light create 3-D images (*see p67*).

Continue to the end of Mercer St, turning right into Canal St.

3   Canal Street

This is the frontier between SoHo and TriBeCa, a vibrant thoroughfare with a

market atmosphere, and stores offering counterfeit luxuries, bargain electronics, photographic equipment, books, and clothing.
Turn right into Greene St.

4 Greene Street

This boasts the city's longest stretch of cast-iron buildings, at Nos 8–34 between Canal and Grand streets. The building at Nos 28–30 is known as the Queen of Greene Street. Built in 1873, it has many of the decorative features which became possible when this new construction method was introduced in the 19th century. The King of Greene Street, at Nos 72–76, is a splendid Renaissance-style building with five floors and an imposing colonnaded porch. A former warehouse and workshop, like all cast-iron buildings in the area, the King today houses art galleries and an up-market antiques shop. On the southwest corner of Prince and Greene streets, the architectural features usually found only on the front of a cast-iron building appear to be continued along the side. But it is only an illusion; look carefully, and you will perceive a mural painted in 1973 by the artist Richard Haas.
Turn left on to Prince St, then right into Wooster St.

5 Wooster Street

Wooster Street is one of the few SoHo thoroughfares still surfaced with the smooth, Belgian-style stone blocks that replaced the earlier cobblestones. At 141 Wooster Street is the New York *Earth Room*, containing a 140-ton sculpture in soil by Walter de Maria. The *Earth Room*

is a permanent exhibit maintained by the non-profit Dia Art Foundation, which also features temporary shows at 77 Wooster Street (between Spring and Broome streets).
Return south along Wooster St, turn right into Broome, then right again on West Broadway.

6 West Broadway

Although it marks the neighbourhood's western edge, West Broadway is unquestionably SoHo's beating heart, especially on Saturday mornings when it is crowded with locals, tourists, and uptown folk. At 393 West Broadway, between Broome and Spring streets, is another Dia Art Foundation permanent exhibit of a work by Walter de Maria. This time it is the *Broken Kilometer*. There are more galleries between Spring and Prince streets.
Continue up West Broadway, turn right into West Houston St, end the walk back at Broadway/Lafayette subway station.

Creative and colourful – an intriguing façade in SoHo

South Street Seaport

A cosy meal at South Street Seaport

Long gone are the days when New York's busy seaport at South Street saw cargo ships sailing off to distant lands. The port's heyday was in the first half of the 19th century, the golden age of sail, when a forest of tall masts lined the East River. It was in the 1860s that trade moved away – some of it to the other side of Manhattan Island, where the deeper water of the Hudson River suited the new steamships. (*See also* Walk *pp92–3.*)

South Street went further and further into decline, its warehouses crumbling, with only the fishing industry and a handful of chandleries continuing in business.

Today, the area has been revitalised as a nautical museum without walls. The 11-block cobblestoned pedestrian-only South Street Seaport Historic District buzzes with activity. Seafood restaurants, shops, bars, piers, craft centres, galleries, and museums draw New Yorkers and visitors alike. Ships of 100 years ago can be visited, and harbour trips enjoyed. In summer, free street entertainment is provided by jugglers, puppeteers, mime artists, jazz groups, and other musicians.

All this has happened since the 1960s, most of the restored area opening to the public in 1983. The development has been one of the city's great commercial successes.

Giving the area added historical significance is the Fulton Fish Market, still going strong after 200 years. The catch is brought in at an unsocial hour, and although the market is open only

between midnight and 8am, dedicated tourists need to get there at dawn to watch the restaurateurs and other wholesale customers buying the harvest of the sea at its freshest. Tours are available.

The restored red-brick warehouses which form Schermerhorn Row date from 1811, and are considered the Seaport's architectural pièce de résistance. The buildings, from Nos 2–18 Fulton Street, 189–195 Front Street, and 91–92 South Street, now contain a variety of novelty shops, restaurants and cafés, and the Seaport Museum Visitors' Center.

All 18 museums at South Street Seaport are housed in renovated buildings. The museum block is on Water Street between Fulton and Beekman streets, where the Seaport Gallery can be found.

More shops, restaurants, and speciality food stores are in the three-storey Fulton Market Building bounded by South, Fulton, Front, and Beekman streets. It was built in 1983 to harmonise with restored properties.

A new Children's Center offers workshops and holiday programmes. At the Maritime Crafts Center, specialists carve intricate wooden figureheads and work on model ships.

The galleries, ships, and restored commercial district which form South Street Seaport Museum, from Water Street to South Street, are open daily throughout the year.

Seven historic ships can be visited at Piers 15 and 16. The *Ambrose* is a small scarlet lightship which once guided steamers into the Port of New York. The *Wavertree* is a three-masted tall ship more than a century old. The *Major Gen William H Hart* is a steam ferry dating from 1925, and the *Lettie G Howard* is the last Gloucester fishing schooner.
South Street Seaport Visitors' Center: 207 Water St. Tel: (212) 732 7678.
Open: daily 10am–5pm.
Subway: Fulton, William St.

The Seaport area by night

The Seaport complex has been completely renovated

Statue of Liberty

Liberty Enlightening the World, better known as the Statue of Liberty, a national monument, is as popular today as she ever was, a universal symbol of democratic freedom. Her size is impressive. She stands 152 feet tall on her 89-foot pedestal, and measures 420 inches around the waist. Her unsmiling mouth is three feet wide.

Emma Lazarus's words, displayed at the site, encapsulate the spirit of Liberty:

Here at our sea-washed sunset gates shall stand A mighty woman with a torch, whose flame Is the imprisoned lightning, and her name Mother of Exiles. From her beacon-hand Glows world-wide welcome; her mild eyes command the air-abridged harbor that twin cities frame. 'Keep ancient lands your storied pomp!' cries she With silent lips. 'Give me your tired, your poor, Your huddled masses yearning to breathe free, The wretched refuse of your teeming shore. Send these, the homeless, tempest-tost to me, I lift my lamp beside the golden door.'

There is almost always a queue for the ferry to Liberty Island, and an irritating bottleneck inside the statue because the elevator can carry only a couple of people at a time (there are also stairs). It goes 10 storeys to the observation deck at the top of the pedestal, a great place for landmark spotting. The physically fit and energetic can leg it a further 12 storeys – up 168 steps – to the crown, but the torch, held aloft 305 feet above sea level, is not open to the public.

Officially, Liberty Island is in New Jersey waters, but the statue has been adjudged to be in New York State, and has a New York City post office address.

The 13½-acre site of the statue has been called Liberty Island since 1956. Originally called Oyster Island, it became Love Island in 1670. In the Revolutionary War it was named Kennedy's Island, and in 1841, when a fort was built on it, it became Fort Wood. The star-shaped wall around the base is part of the former US Fort Wood, and formed part of the defences of New York City between 1841 and 1877. It has also been called Bedloe's Island after Isaac Bedloe, to whom it had once been granted.

In 1986 the statue, which was declared a national monument by President Calvin Coolidge in 1924, underwent a much-needed restoration programme. She had stood for 100 years, and had begun her existence 12 years before that when the French sculptor Frédéric Auguste Bartholdi started to interpret the design of Alexandre Gustave Eiffel, of Eiffel Tower fame.

The French writer Edouard de Laboulaye is credited with having the idea of the statue at the time of the USA centennial in 1876. He felt that the 1778 alliance between France and the USA should be suitably commemorated. Eiffel duly got busy at his drawing board, designing a skeleton of iron, and Bartholdi put on the 'flesh' of ⅛-inch thick hammered copper sheets which were bolted together.

The statue, paid for by the French, took 10 years to build. In 1884 it was dismantled, put into crates, loaded on to the French ship *Isere*, and eventually reassembled and mounted on its pedestal, paid for by the Americans, in 1886. It was dedicated by President Grover Cleveland on 28 October of that year, since when it has been passed by every ship entering New York Harbor. Millions of immigrants have been beckoned into the USA by the statue's 42-foot right arm. Broken shackles lie at her feet, and her left hand holds a law book inscribed 4 July 1776.

Tel: (212) 363 3200.
Open: daily, Jul–Aug 9am–5.30pm; Sep–Jun, 9am–6pm. Closed: 25 Dec.
Subway: 1, 9, N, R to South Ferry.
Bus: M6, M15 to South Ferry, then Circle Line-Statue of Liberty Ferry from the Battery every 30 mins, 9am–3.30pm summer (check for winter hours).
Subway: Currently only 4 & 5 to Bowling Green or N & R to Whitehall.

St Paul's Chapel

Said to be the oldest public building in Manhattan in continuous use since its completion in 1766. This national landmark is where George Washington worshipped, and his pew is one of the things everyone goes to see. Tours of the chapel with its pastel blue and pink interior are by appointment.
Broadway at Fulton & Vesey sts.
Tel: (212) 602 0874. Open: Mon–Fri 9am–3pm, Sun 7am–3pm.
Subway: Fulton St/Broadway.

St Vartan Armenian Cathedral

Modelled on the lines of Armenian architecture of the 5th to 7th centuries, this building contains the Armenian Museum of Art and Antiquities, which has artefacts, art, and manuscripts dating back to the 13th century. There is also a bookstore and gift shop.
2nd Ave at E 34th St.
Tel: (212) 686 0710. Open: daily 9am–6pm. Sun service: 10.30am.
Subway: Park Ave/33rd St.

South Street Seaport Museum

See p77.

Temple Emanu-El

Another New York 'world's largest'. This is the Reform Jewish synagogue in the Upper East Side. It seats 2,500 worshippers. It was built in 1929, influenced by several architectural styles – early Romanesque with Byzantine and Moorish elements, and also a touch of Art Deco.
1 E 65th St. Tel: (212) 744 1400;
www.emanuelnyc.org
Open: Mon–Thu 10am–5pm, Fri
10am–4pm, Sun 10am–7pm.
Subway: Lexington Ave/E 68th St.

Theater District

Historical landmarks still standing include the Byzantine-style Martin Beck Theater, which staged premieres authored by such giants as Eugene O'Neill, Arthur Miller, and Tennessee Williams; the St James, where Lauren Bacall once worked as an usherette; and the Schubert, which witnessed Barbra Streisand's debut in the record-breaking run of *A Chorus Line*. Theater Row, a collection of Off-Broadway playhouses on 42nd Street, between Ninth and Tenth avenues, offers a good choice of productions and eating places.
Subway: Times Square.

TriBeCa

See pp82–3.

Trinity Church

The Anglican parish in Lower Manhattan was established in 1697 by charter from King William III. Public recitals and concerts are held on Tuesday at 12.45pm. The church has a free-entry museum. Tours are given. The present church is the third on the site. Designed by British architect Richard Upjohn, it opened in 1846 before the advent of the skyscraper, and was the tallest building in the city for the next half-century.
Broadway/Wall St. Museum tel: (212) 602 0848; museum tours: (212) 602 0872; www.trinitywallstreet.org
Open: Mon–Fri 7am–6pm, Sat 8am–4pm, Sun 7am–4pm.
Subway: Broadway/Wall St.

The Ukrainian Museum

Masses of hand-painted, vividly coloured *psanky* (Easter eggs); other folk art and ethnic jewellery, ceramics, costumes, and textiles in a small two-storey museum in East Village.
203 2nd Ave/12th St.
Tel: (212) 228 0110;
www.ukrainianmuseum.org
Open: Wed–Sun 1–5pm. Admission charge. Subway: Astor Place.

UNICEF House

Multimedia electronic presentations and an animated giant parrot look at topics such as world peace, global development, and the future. There is a gift shop with greetings cards and other souvenirs.
E 44th St between 1st & 2nd aves.
Tel: (212) 759 0760. Open: Mon–Sat 10am–6pm. Donation suggested.
Subway: Grand Central Station/42nd St.

United Nations Headquarters

See pp84–5.
1st Ave/45th–46th sts. Tel: (212) 963 4440/7713. Open: daily 9.15am–4.45pm; Jan & Feb. Closed: weekends.
Admission charge for guided tours. Free tickets for General Assembly and Councils' meetings 10.30am & 3.30pm (first come first served).
Subway: Grand Central Station.

Vietnam Veterans' Memorial

Excerpts from letters, diary entries, and poems written by Americans who served in the Vietnam War, are etched into this great memorial of granite and green glass blocks. There are also items from news despatches and public statements relating to the war. The memorial is 66 feet long and 16 feet high.
Vietnam Veterans' Plaza, 55 Water St, Lower Manhattan.
Subway: Wall St/William St.

The stirring memorial wall for the dead of the Vietnam War

Walk: TriBeCa

The name TriBeCa has been manufactured from the TRIangle BElow CAnal Street. A former sweatshop area of workshops and warehouses, TriBeCa today is an artistic neighbourhood with fashionable shops and restaurants, and some fine examples of cast-iron buildings. Cheese fanatics should not miss the Cheese of All Nations shop at 153 Chambers Street.

Allow 75 minutes.

Begin from Chambers St/Greenwich St (subway stations at Chambers St/Broadway and also Chambers St/Church St). Proceed up Greenwich St.

1 Greenwich Street

On the left is Washington Market Park, nearly three acres of leisure facilities, on the site of a former food-market area.

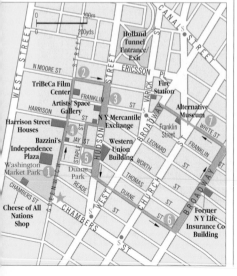

Further along, on the left, opposite Duane Street, is the high-rise Independence Plaza, a residential and commercial complex. At 375 Greenwich Street is the TriBeCa Film Center, a production company partly owned by the actor Robert De Niro, who also has an interest in the street-level restaurant, the TriBeCa Grill, where well-known screen personalities are often seen. On the corner of Greenwich and Harrison streets is a row of 19th-century brick-built houses, moved to this site after being rescued from other parts of the area during demolition in the 1970s. *Continue northwards along Greenwich St. Turn right into North Moore St.*

2 North Moore Street

The fire station at 14 North Moore Street will be familiar to many filmgoers. It was featured prominently in the *Ghostbusters* films. *Turn right into Hudson St.*

3 Hudson Street

The entrance and exits of the Holland Tunnel are located just to the north, between Ericsson Place and Canal Street, and Hudson and Varick streets. It is hard to believe now that this area was once a tranquil park dominated by the Church of St John, and known as Old St John's Square. On the corner of Hudson and Franklin is the Artists' Space Gallery, where works of New York artists are displayed upstairs.

Turn right into Harrison St and left into Staple St.

4 Staple Street

This is where staple products were off-loaded by ships in transit. At the Harrison Street end is the New York Mercantile Exchange, which has the well-known fashionable (and very pricey) French restaurant, Chanterelle, on the ground floor (*see p159*).

Turn left into Jay St and return to Hudson St.

5 Hudson Street

Opposite the end of Jay Street, at No. 60, is the Western Union Building, an Art Deco construction with a façade of bricks in 19 different colours. One block south is Duane Park, a small green area, all that remains of what was a Dutch family farm in the early to mid-1600s. It was acquired by New York City some 200 years ago for a few dollars. Wholesale egg, cheese, and milk businesses are to be found in the area.

Turn left into Duane St and continue east to Broadway. Turn left along Broadway.

6 Broadway

On the corner of Broadway and Leonard Street, the Victorian building which formerly housed the New York Life

Insurance Company is topped by a tall clock tower which was added some 25 years after the offices were erected in 1870. As well as viewing the avant-garde art on display in the Clocktower Gallery, visitors may like to go up into the tower to see the clock's mechanism. There is also a balcony providing a memorable view of New York City.

Continue up Broadway and turn left into White St.

7 White Street

At 17 White Street is the Alternative Museum, where the international social and political scene is boldly illustrated in frequently changed exhibitions of contemporary art. Other cultural activities staged regularly include poetry readings, musical concerts, and recitals.

Continue along White St, turn left along West Broadway to Franklin St subway station.

A zig-zag of fire-escapes in TriBeCa

United Nations

It took a group of architects six years to design the 550-feet high United Nations Building on an 18-acre site. Although geographically located in New York City, the UN headquarters lies in an international zone with its own post office. The guided tour takes an hour (*see p81 for details*). It includes the Secretariat Building, the domed General Assembly Hall, and the Conference Wing.

DINING AT THE UN

The UN Building has a Delegates' Dining Room which members of the public can use for an early lunch. Visitors could find themselves seated at a table next to the UN Secretary General.

If it all seems a little awe-inspiring, just remember that it is not only heads of state and top-name representatives of the nations of the world who gather here. Anyone who has a ticket can attend meetings of the General Assembly and Councils, held between 10.30am and 3.30pm. Tickets are issued free on a first-come-first-served basis, at the information desk in the General Assembly Lobby.

Your next-door neighbour may be sitting in on a deforestation session, or a discussion on war and conflict somewhere in the world. Your local campaigners have probably been represented at debates on nuclear disarmament, dangers to the ozone layer, or problems of developing nations.

The Conference Building houses the Security Council Chamber, the Economic and Social Council, and the Trusteeship Council. Visitors also see a post office where they can buy UN stamps for mail posted in the building. Many post letters to themselves for the sake of the stamp.

The decision to erect the UN Building in New York was made after John D Rockefeller Jr donated $8½ million towards the provision of a permanent site in the city for the headquarters. A team of architects from several nations, led by American Wallace Harrison, combined their talents to design the UN Building between 1947 and 1953. It was completed in 1963.

There are restaurants, shops selling goods from many parts of the world, and a crafts shop. Also worth seeing are works of art donated by member countries, such as the *Reclining Figure*, a bronze statue from the Henry Moore Foundation, the *Statue of Peace* from the former Yugoslavia, and a metal sculpture that depicts a gun with its muzzle tied up to denote peace, which was created by a Swedish artist. Beautiful rose gardens on the 18-acre site overlook the East River.

The organisation developed from the pre-war League of Nations, which had failed to prevent World War II and was disbanded in 1946. During the war Britain, the USA, the Soviet Union, France, and China got together with a view to forming a new world organisation.

On New Year's Day 1942, the representatives of 26 countries signed

Flags of member nations of the UN flutter in harmony in the International Zone

the Declaration of the United Nations in Washington DC, but it was not until April 1945 that the UN was officially founded, at the Conference on Inter-national Organisation in San Francisco, when representatives of 50 nations unanimously adopted the UN Charter.

In that same month, US President Franklin D Roosevelt died. His widow, Eleanor, was to chair the UN Commission on Human Rights from 1947 to 1951.

The first Secretary General of the United Nations was Trygve Lie, a Norwegian politician, elected in 1946 on 1 February. He held the office until 1952. Today, a total of 189 states have UN membership.

Four purposes are listed in the UN Charter: to maintain international peace and security; to encourage friendly relations between states, based on the principle of equal rights and self-determination for all; to promote international co-operation in solving social, economic, and cultural problems; and to serve as an agency through which member states can act to achieve these goals.

Business is conducted in six official languages – Arabic, Chinese, English, French, Russian, and Spanish.

Villard Houses

A must for architecture-spotters, these three brownstone mansions date from 1886, and were built in palazzo-style for newspaper publisher Henry Villard. The buildings form an early Renaissance-style courtyard with elaborate wrought iron, and are now integrated with the Helmsley Palace Hotel. The interiors are in pristine condition.
Madison Ave/50th St.
Subway: Lexington Ave/51st St.

Waldorf-Astoria Hotel

As much a part of New York as the Empire State Building or the Statue of Liberty, the 1,692-room Waldorf-Astoria is an Art Deco masterpiece in its own right. This was where the Waldorf salad was invented. The hotel still draws the rich and famous – as well as honeymoon couples from Middle America – and its luxurious lobby continues to be a major meeting point.
301 Park Ave. Tel: (212) 355 3000.
Subway: Grand Central Station.

Whitney Museum of American Art

There is always something exciting to see here, especially in alternate years (those with odd numbers) in the spring, when the exhibitions pinpoint what new things are happening on the American art scene. The Whitney, founded in 1930 by Gertrude Vanderbilt Whitney, concentrates on the 20th century. Its galleries display a variety of styles and themes from a wide range of artists. There are changing exhibitions, and film and video programmes are presented.

If you wait long enough, you might spot someone famous here

945 Madison Ave/75th St.
Tel: (212) 570 3676; www.whitney.org
Open: Tue–Thu 11am–6pm, Fri 1–9pm,
Sat & Sun 11am–6pm. Closed: Mon,
Independence Day, Christmas Day, & New
Year's Day. Admission charge (free Tue
evening; Fri 6–9pm pay what you wish).
Subway: Lexington Ave/77th St.

There are Whitney Museum branches at
three other Manhattan locations:

Whitney Museum Downtown

Five annual exhibitions of
contemporary American art and regular
Gallery talks.
Federal Reserve Plaza, 33 Maiden Lane/
Nassau St. Tel: (212) 943 5655.
Open: Mon–Fri 11am–6pm.
Free admission. Subway: Broad St.

Whitney Museum at Equitable Center

A 68-foot high mural by Roy
Lichtenstein greets visitors entering the
atrium. Murals by Thomas Hart Benton
depict American life between the two
World Wars. Two major collections on
show, one frequently changed.
787 7th Ave between 51st & 52nd sts.
Tel: (212) 554 1113. Open: Mon–Fri
11am–6pm, Thu 11am–7.30pm, Sat
noon–5pm. Free admission.
Subway: 6th Ave/50th St.

Whitney Museum at Philip Morris

Small picture gallery, with changing
exhibitions on modern themes, and a
sculpture court.
120 Park Ave/42nd St. Tel: (212) 878
2550. Open: Mon–Sat 11am–6pm, Thu
11am–7.30pm. Sculpture court open:
Mon–Sat 7.30am–9.30pm, Sun 4–7pm.

Free admission. Subway: Grand Central
Station/42nd St.

Woolworth Building

Dubbed the 'Cathedral of Commerce',
the 792-foot white terracotta building
was the world's tallest when it opened in
1913. It was the headquarters of the
Woolworth corporation, whose founder,
Frank Woolworth, made a fortune from
the chain of 'nickel and dime' stores in
which all merchandise was originally
sold for either 5 or 10 cents. Many
architecture students regard the building
as the pinnacle of achievement in the
genre. Its graceful lines are decorated
with extravagant Gothic-style detail, and
its lobby is not to be missed. Sculpted
reliefs in the four corners of the lobby
include one of Woolworth counting out
nickels and dimes with which to pay the
architect Gilbert, who has a model of
the building in his arms.
Broadway/Park Place.
Subway: City Hall.

World Financial Center

New York's newest residential and
commercial community, Battery Park
City, is dominated by the World
Financial Center, and occupies a site
alongside the Hudson River (*see* Walk
pp90–91). The urban dream of a new
city-within-a-city in Lower Manhattan,
with office towers for international
financial concerns and homes for 30,000
people, was formulated in the 1960s,
designed by architects Cesar Pelli &
Associates, and opened in 1988. Today, it
is all in place, within a short walk of
Wall Street.
    Battery Park City was drastically

affected by the September 2001 terrorist attacks on the neighbouring World Trade Center. Nonetheless, the area has bounced back as a resilient home for many, and a city-within-a-city as the nearby Ground Zero site continues to be excavated. The surrounding area is in a state of flux, with visitors more welcome in some areas than others.

200 Liberty St, on West St, between Liberty/Vesey sts. Tel: (212) 945 2600. www.worldfinancialcenter.com

Yeshiva University Museum

Dramatic exhibits on Jewish history and art. Special events, live performances, films, and holiday workshops.

2520 Amsterdam Ave/185th St (Campus Gallery). Tel: (212) 960 5390. Open: Tue–Thu 10am–5pm; Sun noon–6pm. Closed: Aug. Subway: 181st St. Main galleries at Center for Jewish

World Financial Centre Building

History: 15W 16th St. Tel: (212) 294 8330. Open: Tue, Wed, & Sun 11am–5pm, Thu 11am–8pm. Admission charge. Guided tours by appointment.

Yorkville

See Walk, pp98–9.

Jewish art and history celebrated at the Yeshiva University Museum

Ground Zero

Until they were tragically destroyed on 11 September 2001 in terrorist attacks by two suicidal jet airliners, the World Trade Center (WTC) twin towers towered over the Manhattan skyline as a symbol of the dynamic New York metropolis. More than 24 acres of Battery Park City's 92 acres were scooped out of the earth in creating the Center.

Built by the Port Authority of New York and New Jersey, and its international headquarters, WTC was best known for its 110-storey-high twin towers. On a clear day, the open-air rooftop viewing point was the best place to view the city and had more than a quarter of a million visitors a year. Each tower was served by 23 high-speed lifts controlled by computer, and able to reach the top in less than a minute. The towers played a starring role in the remake of *King Kong*.

For 50,000 people the towers were a workplace, housing at least 1,200 firms, representing more than 60 countries. At least 80,000 people visited on business every weekday.

The Center was served by 22 restaurants, cafés, and snack bars, the most famous being the Windows on the World Restaurant at Observation Deck level. At concourse level was an indoor shopping mall.

The concept of a World Trade Center was born in the late 1950s, in a bid to resurrect what was a depressed area. The first tenants moved into one of the towers in 1970, and the Center was dedicated in 1973. During the peak construction period there were 3,500 workers involved in the perilous job of erecting the towers.

At the time of writing, a viewing deck at Ground Zero has been created for those wishing to view the site. Future plans for the site, including a memorial or rebuilding, are still under discussion. Areas restricted to the public are clearly designated.

Observation Deck: Broadway and Fulton St. Tickets are required and are distributed free of charge at the South Street Seaport Museum booth on Pier 16 on a first-come-first-serve basis in half hour slots (noon–8pm) or for the next day (9–11.30am). The ticket booth opens 11am–6pm (tel: (212) SEAPORT).

Walk: Battery Park – Financial District

New York's Financial District, containing one of the world's most famous thoroughfares, is at the southerly tip of Manhattan Island. Early skyscrapers vie for attention with modern ones in the district's skyline.

Allow 2 hours.

Begin from Staten Island Ferry Terminal (South Ferry subway station) and head west into Battery Park (see p30), staying close to the water's edge.

1 Battery Park

Named after the line of cannon which once defended the old shoreline (now State Street), the park has lots of statuary and welcome greenery. Landfill has extended the area much further into the sea than it used to be. The steps of

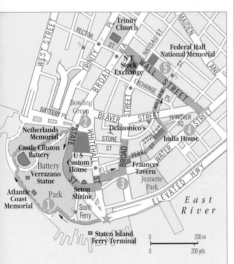

the **Atlantic Coast Memorial**, a monument commemorating US servicemen who died in World War II, offer a splendid view of New York Harbor, including such sights as Staten Island, Ellis Island, and the Statue of Liberty. Also in the Park is Castle Clinton (*see p31*), a circular, brick-built fortress which was on an island 200 feet offshore when it was built in 1811. It now houses a museum, with a ticket office for ferries to Ellis and Liberty islands.

In Battery Park is a statue of Giovanni da Verrazano, who sailed into New York Harbor in 1524. Letters from men and women who served in the US forces are etched in glass at the Vietnam Veterans' Memorial in Jeanette Park, off Water Street (*see p81*).

From Castle Clinton walk inland along the broad mall, passing the Netherlands Memorial, commemorating the exchange of beads that purchased Manhattan from the Indians in 1626, and leave the park at State St.

2 Bowling Green

On the opposite side of State Street is the ornate **US Custom House**, built in 1907 on the site of the old Fort Amsterdam, now the **Museum of the**

Native American. Statuary symbolising the various continents was sculpted by Daniel Chester French, who created President Abraham Lincoln's statue at the Lincoln Memorial in Washington DC. The Custom House stands opposite Bowling Green, opened in 1773 as New York's first public park. The statue of Britain's King George III here was toppled and melted down for bullets soon after the American Declaration of Independence in July 1776.
Head south (right) along State St, passing the shrine of St Elizabeth Ann Seton, the first American-born saint. Turn left in Water St, then left again at Broad St.

3 Broad Street
This is where New York's past and present converge. Interspersed among the glitz of modern commerce are pre-Independence relics. At Pearl and Broad streets is **Fraunces Tavern Museum** (*see pp52–3*), a three-storey Georgian brick building where George Washington bade his troops farewell in 1783. The course of the old Stone Street, built by the Dutch, is marked by a line of paving stones in the lobby of a modern office complex at 85 Broad Street. At the side of this building, in Pearl Street, you can peep through a glass panel in the pavement to see the foundations of the old Dutch City Hall.
From Pearl St head away from Broad St to reach Hanover Square.

4 Hanover Square
Another vintage location: the first printing press in the American colonies was established here, and Captain Kidd was once a resident. India House, former site of the New York Cotton Exchange, now houses the classic downtown bar, Harry's of Hanover Square. To the west, where Hanover Square meets Beaver and South William streets, is Delmonico's restaurant, originally opened in 1827.
Continue up William St, turn left into Wall St.

5 Wall Street
The golden gulch, Wall Street (*see pp92–3*) cleaves through the skyscrapers for barely a third of a mile – at one end, a narrow view of the East River, at the other, Trinity Church, dwarfed by financial powerhouses. Wall Street follows the line of a wooden wall built by the Dutch to keep the native Americans and British trade rivals at bay. A statue of George Washington on the steps of the Federal Hall National Memorial at Wall and Nassau streets, marks the spot where the first US president was sworn in. The New York Stock Exchange has a visitor centre and gallery. Trinity Church, once the city's tallest building, dates from 1846. It is the third church on the site, and its charter goes back to 1697 (*see p44*).

Workers in the Financial District take a breather in Battery Park

Wall Street has become synonymous with New York's Financial District, which in fact extends outwards from Wall Street. Wall Street actually leads a schizophrenic life. At weekends, tourism rules. The skyscraper office blocks are empty and visitors are free to amble along, noting the more important buildings. On weekdays, any tourist strolling along the sidewalk is likely to be mown down by speeding pedestrians. The local business fraternity, smartly suited, clips along at a frantic pace, overtaking the crawling cabs and limos. Everyone is busy-busy-busy, and essential inter-office activity has to be completed as quickly as possible. The implication is that if the sidewalks were less crowded, the Wall Street population would take to roller skates or skateboards. As it is, upwardly mobile young Titans grab a 20-minute lunch break, change into shorts, shirt, and trainers like inflatable boats, and jog their way through the throng.

The frenzied pace of Wall Street's present lifestyle could not be in greater contrast to the area's beginnings in 1792, when a group of stock dealers signed the Buttonwood Agreement, a quaint name taken from the trees under which

Fortunes are won and lost in Wall Street's financial institutions

they used to conduct their business in those leisurely days. Today's brokers work on the verge of panic, snapping into their telephones, stabbing at computer keyboards with nervous fingers, casting neurotic eyes at screens full of figures, and drowning themselves, it seems, in a rising tide of scrap paper. Tourists can relax and enjoy the spectacle from the visitors' gallery at the New York Stock Exchange (see p70), between New and Broad streets, watching the frenzy build up as those on the floor do their darnedest to squeeze and pinch as they wheel and deal.

A short walk away is the World Financial Center (see pp87–8). Other major financial institutions in the vicinity include the Renaissance-style Federal Reserve Bank, the Chase Manhattan Bank and Plaza, famous for its *Four Trees* Jean Dubuffet sculpture, and the 1932 Irving Trust Company.

Life is hard in high finance, and you have to keep fit to keep going. Some of them do it by taking a brief breather for spiritual refreshment at a free lunchtime concert at Trinity Church. Then, when the working day is over, the commuters pile into the bars and eateries of South Street Seaport, Chambers Street, and Beaver Street, getting up their strength to face the homeward bridge-and-tunnel journey. This is their happy hour.

Walk: St Paul's Chapel– South Street Seaport

This part of Lower Manhattan takes in the old skyscraper district, starting from where the World Trade Center once stood, and including the Woolworth Building, the courts, and the restored waterfront on the East River.

Allow 2 hours.

Begin on Fulton St and Broadway. Head northwards and turn right on Fulton St, and then left to reach Broadway.

1 Broadway

St Paul's Chapel, on the corner of Broadway and Fulton Street, dates from 1766, and is Manhattan's oldest surviving

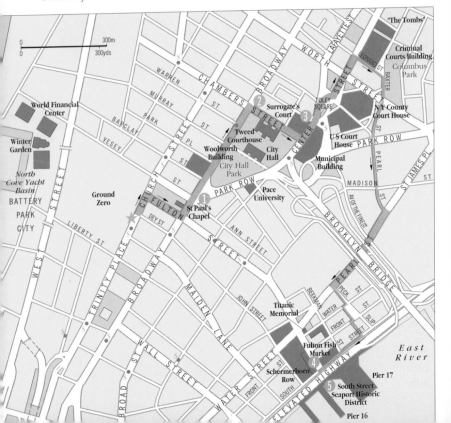

church. Modelled after St Martin-in-the-Fields, London, St Paul's was where George Washington worshipped, and where he prayed after his inauguration as president. At Park Place and Broadway is the 792-foot Woolworth Building, the world's tallest when it opened in 1913 as the headquarters of the Woolworth empire. Opposite is City Hall Park, or the old town common. Recently renovated, the park boasts a wonderful ground etching chronicling New York City's history.

Continue up Broadway and turn right into Chambers St.

2 Chambers Street

This is the start of New York's 'Court Quarter'. On the right is the Tweed Courthouse, completed in 1878 at the then phenomenal cost of $12 million; its creator, politician William Marcy Tweed, was driven from office for corruption. Further along Chambers Street, on the left, is the ornate Surrogate's Court, also known as the Hall of Records.

Turn left into Center St.

3 Center Street

Across Center Street is the Municipal Building, built in 1914 as the city government's first skyscraper. Happy-looking New Yorkers leaving the building have just obtained marriage licences. Center Street veers right at Foley Square, where marble steps lead to the imposing entrance of the US Court House. Topped with a gilded pyramid, the building has witnessed many famous trials. Across Center Street is the hexagonal New York County Court House, in which the film *Twelve Angry Men* was shot.

Turn right on Leonard St, right into Baxter St, then cross Worth St to Cardinal Hayes Place and Pearl St. Follow Pearl under Brooklyn Bridge and turn left into Peck Slip. Follow your nose to the waterfront and Fulton Fish Market!

4 Fulton Fish Market

Despite many attempts to relocate them, fishmongers have been selling catches here since before the War of Independence (*see p76*).

Continue along South St to the South Street Seaport.

5 South Street Seaport

Covering 11 blocks, the South Street Seaport Historic District was created from restored waterfront buildings and piers in 1967 (*see pp76–7*). Historic ships, including the square-rigged *Peking*, are docked at Pier 16. The visitor centre is on the ground floor of Schermerhorn Row, a terrace of red-brick warehouses.

Best view of the Hudson is from the Winter Garden Atrium, World Financial Center.

Street sculpture on Broadway

W a l k : Y o r k v i l l e

Yorkville, Upper East Side, retains much of its Central European character – immigrants from Germany, Austria, Hungary, and the former Czechoslovakia have been settled here since the 1870s. There are beer halls, delicatessens and pastry shops, and restaurants serving Wiener schnitzel and red cabbage.

Allow 1½ hours.

Begin at E 86th St subway station. Walk briskly or catch a bus the half mile to the eastern end of E 86th St.

1 Henderson Place Historic District

Located between York Avenue and East End Avenue, Henderson Place has a row of 24 small, turreted Queen Anne-style cottages of brick and timber, built as servants' quarters in 1882, and now among the city's most desirable residences. The servants' employers lived in nearby mansions which have long since vanished.

Cross East End Ave to Carl Schurz Park.

2 Carl Schurz Park

Overlooking the East River, the park affords a view of the Triborough Bridge and Hell's Gate, where treacherous currents of the Harlem River, Long Island Sound, and New York Harbor merge. On the opposite side of the river is the borough of Queens. The park honours a versatile German immigrant who served as a US diplomat, a Union Army major general, and a senator representing Missouri. Appointed Secretary of the Interior in President John Quincy Adams's government, he

also later became editor of *Harper's Weekly.* He died in 1906.

Walk north through the park to Gracie Mansion.

3 Gracie Mansion

Built in the late 18th century, Gracie Mansion was the home of wealthy merchant Archibald Gracie. The City of New York acquired it in 1887, using it as a museum. Since the 1930s when the popular Fiorello LaGuardia resided here, it has been the official residence of the Mayor of New York.

Leave Carl Schurz Park at E 88th St and head west.

4 East 88th Street

Between First and Second avenues is the French Gothic-style Church of the Holy Trinity – flying buttresses, arches, gargoyles, and stained-glass windows in the style of the Middle Ages. Organ recitals and concerts of classical music are presented in the church. Between Park and Fifth avenues, 88th Street marks the southern border of the Carnegie Hill area, one of the city's most exclusive residential neighbourhoods. The area is named after millionaire

Andrew Carnegie, who set a trend – followed by the Astors and Vanderbilts – by building a mansion in what were the unfashionable northern outskirts of Manhattan in 1901.

Continue west on E 88th St, then turn right into 5th Ave.

5 Fifth Avenue

This part of Fifth Avenue is known as Museum Mile. It stretches from the Frick Collection at 70th Street to El Museo del Barrio at 105th Street. Frank Lloyd Wright's controversial spiral building, the Guggenheim Museum between 88th and 89th streets, presents an unusual, exciting, and practical way of looking at art. The museum's six floors (pedants will say there is just one, wound like a watchspring) display works by Chagall, Klee, and Picasso.

Next, on 89th/90th, comes the National Academy of Design, an elegant mansion housing a collection of American art. At 91st Street is the Smithsonian Institution's National Museum of Design, better known as the Cooper-Hewitt Museum. This is the 64-room mansion built by Andrew Carnegie. A block north is the Jewish Museum. At 94th Street is the International Center of Photography.

Turn right on to E 96th St and end the walk at the 96th St subway.

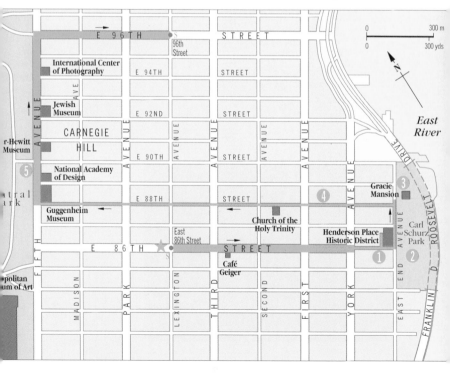

The West End of the early 19th century comprised small distinct villages, and remained largely undeveloped. It was the coming of the subway that enhanced its appeal and urbanised it through the proliferation of apartment blocks.

In the 1890s, Columbia University relocated here. Artists

and academics shared the neighbour-hood with the equally lively mob, which played and fought its flashy way through the early decades of the 20th century. Development and construction ceased from the early 1930s through to the early 1980s and the Upper West Side's popularity waned, making it an undesirable address.

A fearsome reputation spread swiftly

when the film version of Leonard Bernstein's musical *West Side Story* (based on the Romeo and Juliet theme) burst on to the wide screens of the world in 1960. The menacing glint of knives, defiant young toughs strutting the decaying streets and spoiling for a fight – images of poverty, degradation, and violence were conveyed with gritty realism. But the film was also an epitaph for the area it portrayed. The streets in which many of the scenes were actually shot were already condemned, and when the camera crews moved out the bulldozers moved in. The mouldering tenements and sweatshops, the rubble-strewn battlefields that were once playgrounds, the dyeing shops and

schools, were all razed to make way for the splendour of the Lincoln Center, the main aim of which was to raise the tone of the area.

Today's West Side story is one of culture and multi-ethnic coexistence. There are still some slums, but in the main the area bordered by Central

Park on the east, the Hudson River on the west, and by 59th and 114th streets to the south and north, is comfortable and safe, with trendy boutiques and restaurants, and smart apartment blocks.

It seems that the Upper West Side is now settling into the intended lifestyle of a place which has attracted as residents the likes of Thomas Wolfe, Enrico Caruso, Igor Stravinsky, Arturo Toscanini, John Lennon, Yoko Ono, and many other luminaries.

Far removed from its 1960s reputation for violence, the West Side today is marked by its colourful multi-ethnic society and institutions such as the Lincoln Center (left); and the American Museum of Natural History (right)

The Bronx

A Danish immigrant, Johannes Bronck, founded the Bronx when he bought 500 acres of land from the Dutch West India Company in 1639. The only borough connected to the mainland, the Bronx was originally inhabited by the wealthy, but through the decades gradually acquired a rather run-down reputation. Its population is about one and a quarter million, now comprising several ethnic groups who settled here. A large community of Italians live in the Belmont area.

Reaching up for a tasty snack of creepy crawlies

Unless you are in the crowd at the Yankee Stadium and the right team wins, or at the Zoo, where the animals live in something like their natural habitat, you do not go to the Bronx specifically to be cheered and uplifted. Indeed, one of the local attractions is a cemetery, and another is the cottage where Edgar Allan Poe spent a sad time towards the end of his life.

On the other hand, if you disregard the warnings of New Yorkers, you can explore much of the Bronx in complete safety and feel rewarded for the effort. The Zoo and Wave Hill – a former estate – and the New York Botanical Garden are green havens. Where else have you ever come across a snuff mill?

To get to these delights, take the subway and travel right through the South Bronx – the trains come out into the daylight here. More northerly parts have gained favour in recent years as a place to set up home.

The one part of the South Bronx that draws New Yorkers by the thousand is the **Yankee Stadium** – the first subway station reached from Manhattan. The Yankees baseball team moved from Harlem to the Bronx in 1923. Team stalwart Babe Ruth played for the Yankees for 15 years, and his statue, along with those of other greats like Joe DiMaggio, can be seen at the stadium.

Arthur Avenue Retail Market
A marketplace with several dozen stalls. Fruit and vegetables are piled high and big cheeses and strings of spicy sausages dangle temptingly before the eyes. *2344 Arthur Ave.*

Bartow-Pell Mansion
Built between 1836 and 1842, the mansion is preserved as a historical museum and national landmark. There are several hiking trails in the park. *Pelham Bay Park. Tel: (718) 885 1461. Open: Wed, Sat, Sun noon–4pm. Closed: last three weeks of Aug. Admission charge.*

Bronx Heritage Trail
Guided tours of three historical houses.

Bronx County Historical Society, 3309
Bainbridge Ave. Tel: (718) 881 8900.
Open: Sat 10am–4pm, Sun 1–5pm,
weekdays by appointment.

Bronx Museum of the Arts

Permanent art exhibits ranging from
Old Masters to new local talent, as well
as changing exhibitions.
1040 Grand Concourse/165th St.
Tel: (718) 681 6000.
Open: Wed 3–9pm, Thu & Fri
10am–5pm, Sat & Sun 1–6pm.
Donation suggested.
Subway: 161st St/Grand Concourse.

Bronx Supreme Court House

This was one of the locations for the
film *Bonfire of the Vanities.*
Subway: Grand Concourse.

Bronx Zoo
(New York Zoological Gardens)

The largest urban zoo in the USA, with
nearly 4,000 creatures covering nearly
700 species on 265 acres. The animals
enjoy simulated indoor and outdoor
habitats, like Jungle World, a glass-
enclosed mangrove swamp and tropical
rainforest environment, with clouds and
waterfalls. There are also Himalayan
Highlands, with snow leopard and
panda, African Plains, Wolf Woods, a
World of Darkness (with nocturnal
animals), a World of Birds, a mouse
house, and a huge wilderness area

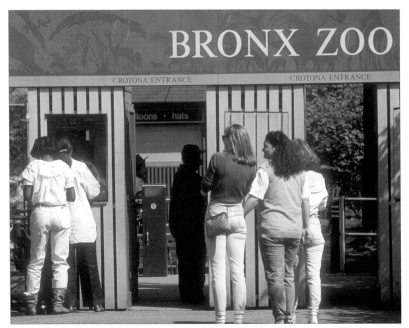

A day at the zoo – popular with all ages

devoted to the tigers and elephants of Wild Asia which can be seen from the Bengali Express monorail and the Safari cable car from May to October.
Bronx River Parkway/Fordham Rd.
Tel: (718) 367 1010.
Open: weekdays 10am–5pm,
weekends 10am–5.30pm.
Admission charge Thu–Tue;
donation suggested on Wed.
Subway: East Tremont Ave.

City Island
Set in Long Island Sound, off the borough's eastern shore, this is a fishing, boatbuilding, and yachting community, with an assortment of seafood restaurants. There are gingerbread houses, bungalows with stained-glass windows, and an historical nautical museum at 190 Fordham Road. A narrow causeway connects the island with Pelham Bay Park. Several yachts entered for the America's Cup, including the *Intrepid,* a winner in the 1960s, are moored here.
Nautical Museum. Tel: (718) 885 0701.
Open: weekdays noon–3pm, Sat
10am–3pm. Closed: Sun.
Admission charge.

Enrico Fermi Cultural Center
Housed within the Belmont branch of New York City Library. Books on the achievements and contributions of Italian immigrants to local life can be found in the Heritage Collection here.
610 E 186th St. Tel: (718) 933 6410.
Subway: Fordham Rd.

Fordham University
Formerly a self-contained village, now skirting the Grand Concourse, Fordham has been settled over the past 150 years by Irish, Germans, Italians, Jews, blacks, Hispanics, and, more recently, refugees from Cambodia and Albania. Today, Fordham University, on an 85-acre site near the Botanical Garden, is one of several campuses in the Bronx and has 7,500 students. The university dates back to 1841, the dominant building being a massive pile, Keating Hall.
Subway: Fordham Rd.

Hall of Fame for Great Americans
Noted Americans of the past from many walks of life are commemorated in this granite colonnade designed by Stanford White. The landmark structure houses busts of presidents, statesmen, scientists, artists, and humanitarians.
   Tours can be booked in advance.
Bronx Community College, 181st
St/University Ave. Tel: (718) 289 5161.
Open: daily 10am–5pm. Free admission.
Subway: Bedford Park Blvd/Lehman
College.

Lehman College for the Performing Arts
A major entertainment centre for music, dance, and theatre.
Bedford Park Blvd. Tel: (718) 960 8833.
Box office: (718) 960 8732.
Subway: Bedford Park Blvd/Lehman
College.

Museum of Bronx History
See Valentine-Varian House (p105).

New York Botanical Garden
Inspired by Kew Gardens during a visit to England in 1889, botanists Dr

Nathaniel Lord and his wife Elizabeth Britton returned to New York determined to create something similar. In only two years, with a deep gorge of the Bronx River and 40 acres of original woodland providing special features, the basics were completed. Today, 11 splendid galleries form the **Enid A Haupt Conservatory**, with orchids, ferns, palms, cacti, and flowers of the tropics. Another building on the 250-acre site is the 1840 Lorillard Snuff Mill, where tobacco was ground for snuff, with the petals of roses growing nearby contributing to the blend. The museum building houses a herbarium, with many thousands of dried plants. There is also a library and a garden shop where visitors can obtain a guide to the gardens. The Erph Compass Garden, with cobblestones marking the points of the compass, is just one of the brilliant collections of flowers.

Southern Blvd south of Mosholu Parkway in Bronx Park, adjacent to Bronx Zoo. Tel: (718) 817 8700; www.nybg.org Open: Nov–Mar, Tue–Sun 10am–6pm; Apr–Oct, daily 10am–6pm. Admission charge. Enid A Haupt Conservatory has an admission charge (free on Sat mornings, Apr–Oct). Subway: Bedford Park Blvd/Grand Concourse.

The Botanical Garden provides a welcome sense of country tranquillity

Yankee Stadium, the Bronx, focus of big league games

NEW YORK IN BLOOM

Special flower displays are held at various times of the year at the New York Botanical Garden in the Bronx. First is a spring bulb show in February, followed by a daffodil and magnolia weekend in early April. April also brings the New York Orchid Show. A bonsai exhibition is held in October.

North Wind Undersea Museum

Hands-on displays of deep-sea diving equipment and marine mammal rescue, with films of the Whale Rescue Team at work. Other attractions include demonstrations of harbour seals working with deep sea divers, exhibits of scrimshaw (the engraving of whalebone and teeth) and recovered sunken treasure, submarines, and diving bells. In fact, the entrance itself is made from the nine-foot gaping jaws of a whale.
610 City Island Ave, City Island.
Tel: (718) 885 0701. Open: weekdays 10am–5pm, weekends noon–5pm.

Pelham Bay Park

More than 2,000 acres of land form Pelham Bay Park, part of a tract bought from the Native Americans by Thomas Pell in 1654. There is a mile of beach, a riding school and boat basin, and facilities for cycling, picnicking, fishing, and tennis.

Poe Cottage

Edgar Allan Poe moved here from Manhattan with his sick wife, Virginia, in the hope that her health would improve, but she succumbed to tuberculosis. Her death bed and his rocking chair are in the sparsely furnished cottage where Poe lived for three years. After moving out from here, Poe soon died under mysterious circumstances.
East Kingsbridge Rd/Grand Concourse.
Tel: (718) 881 8900.
Open: Sat 10am–4pm, Sun 1–5pm.
Closed: Mon–Fri. Admission charge.
Subway: Kingsbridge Rd.

Riverdale

In contrast to South Bronx, this is a region above University Heights overlooking the Hudson River and the New Jersey Palisades, where wealthy 19th-century Manhattanites built spacious summer homes.

Valentine-Varian House

Fieldstone farmhouse built by blacksmith Isaac Valentine in 1758. It houses the Museum of Bronx History. *3266 Bainbridge Ave/E 208th St. Tel: (718) 881 8900. Open: for weekday tours by appointment, Sat 10am–4pm, Sun 1–5pm. Admission charge.*

Van Cortlandt Park

West Indian immigrants play cricket in this extensive park in the northwest of the Bronx, part of a 1646 Dutch land grant. Golf, tennis, riding, boating, and other recreational facilities are available.

Wave Hill

A Riverdale area estate of 28 acres bought in 1903 by George W Perkins. It has been home at different times to Mark Twain, Theodore Roosevelt, and Arturo Toscanini. A manor house dates from 1844. Perkins built another, and created gardens with greenhouses, rare plants, and a sculpture garden. Concerts are performed here. *675 W 252nd St. Tel: (718) 549 3200. www.wavehill.org Open: Tue–Sun 9am–5pm (summer); 9am–4.30pm (fall & winter). Free admission before noon, Tue–Sat.*

Woodlawn Cemetery

Spot the famous names in this 130-year-old cemetery with some over-the-top edifices – a *Who's Where* guide can be obtained at the cemetery office. Duke Ellington is here,

and so is FW Woolworth in an Egyptian-style palace. *233rd St/Webster Ave. Tel: (718) 920 0500. Open: daily 9.30am–4.30pm. Free admission. Subway: Woodlawn.*

Yankee Stadium

Home of the New York Yankees baseball team, and hailed as one of the nation's finest sports facilities, it was built in 1923 by Jacob Ruppert, owner of the Yankees. The stadium has a seating capacity of 54,000.

161st St/ River Ave. Tel: (718) 293 6000. Office open: Mon–Sat 9am–5pm; Sun 10am– 5pm. Subway: Yankee Stadium.

Baseball is a national obsession

At first there were only what they now call 'Native Americans', aloof, inscrutable – and cunning enough to trade for a bargain price an island (Manhattan) that did not belong to them. They made way for the Dutch, who soon allowed the British on the scene. After the Revolution, independent America opened its doors and New York's ethnic diversification accelerated. In the mid-19th century came the mass waves of European migration into New York, caused by the social upheaval of the Napoleonic wars, the potato famines in Ireland and Germany, and the unsettling effects of the Industrial Revolution. Initially, the Irish and German immigrants pre-dominated, but by the early 1900s, Jews and Italians were the largest groups.

The descendants of New York's original immigrants – the Dutch, English, and Germans – are hard to find nowadays, although Yorkville still has a strong German flavour. The Irish, too, are scattered, but there are enclaves still in parts of Queens and the Bronx.

Close-knit Jewish communities

are to be found in the Bronx, Brooklyn, and Queens, with sizeable groupings of the strictly Orthodox Hasidic Jews in Williamsburg, Crown Heights, and Borough Park in Brooklyn. Of the once-teeming Jewish community on Manhattan's Lower East Side, only a few remnants remain. Many Italian-Americans, too, have moved to the suburbs, but the city still has a number of recognisable neighbourhoods. Once threatened by encroachment from adjoining Chinatown, Little Italy has managed to maintain its identity and continues to thrive.

The variety of eating and other commercial establishments testify to the rich mix of cultures found in New York: a restaurant in the 86th Street German area (facing page); a bookshop for Hungarian readers (right); and Little Italy (below)

Brooklyn

With two and a half million inhabitants – almost double those in Manhattan – Brooklyn is the largest of the five boroughs in terms of population. Many visitors get no further than elegant Brooklyn Heights, unless they take a trip to Coney Island or Brighton Beach, but the borough's attractions are well worth exploring.

Jogging on Brooklyn Esplanade

Borough Hall
Brooklyn's seat of government is a sober Greek Revival building, part of the Brooklyn Heights civic centre. Tours are led by an architectural historian.
209 Joralemon St. Tel: (718) 875 4047. Open: Tue 1pm for tours only. Free admission. Subway: Borough Hall.

Brighton Beach
Situated at the eastern end of Coney Island, the resort is known as 'Little Odessa' because it is home to some 30,000 Russian émigrés, the largest such community in the USA, many of whom arrived during the 1970s. There is lots of noisy vodka drinking, and Georgian menus in inexpensive restaurants.
Subway: Brighton Beach.

Brooklyn Academy of Music
Founded in 1859, BAM, as aficionados call it, is an outstanding cultural centre, with four theatres.
30 Lafayette Ave. Tel: (718) 636 4100. Subway: Atlantic Ave or Pacific St.

Brooklyn Botanic Garden
Covering 52 acres and noted for its Japanese, fragrance, and herb gardens.
1000 Washington Ave. Tel: (718) 623

7200; www.bbg.org Open: Oct–Mar, Tue–Fri 8am–4.30pm, Sat, Sun, & holidays 10am–4.30pm; Apr–Sep, Tue–Fri 8am–6pm, Sat, Sun, & holidays 10am–6pm. Subway: Botanic Gardens.

Brooklyn Bridge
Opened in 1883, the bridge was one of the finest Victorian engineering achievements, and still ranks among the world's greatest suspension spans. Superb views from its upper walkway.
Subway: High St/Brooklyn Bridge.

Brooklyn Children's Museum
Lots of hands-on experiences and more than 40,000 authentic ethnological, natural history, and other artefacts.
*145 Brooklyn Ave. Tel: (718) 735 4432; www.fieldtrip.com
Open: Wed–Fri 2–5pm, Sat & Sun noon–5pm. Donation suggested. Subway: Kingston/Throop aves.*

Brooklyn Heights Historic District
A 50-block area reflecting the architectural styles of 19th-century America. (See Walk pp110–11).
Walk across Brooklyn Bridge from Lower Manhattan, or ride the subway to Brooklyn Bridge/High St or Clark St.

Brooklyn History Museum
Located in the Brooklyn Heights Historic District, the museum features Brooklyn Dodgers' baseball exhibits, and displays on Coney Island, Brooklyn Bridge, and Brooklyn Navy Yard.
128 Pierrepont St, Brooklyn Heights, at the corner of Clinton St & Pierrepont St. Tel: (718) 624 0890.
Open: Tue–Sat noon–5pm.
Admission charge. Subway: Clark St.

Brooklyn Museum of Art
One of the nation's leading museums. The Egyptian collection is said to be even finer than those in Cairo and the British Museum in London.
200 Eastern Parkway. Tel: (718) 638 5000. Open: Wed–Fri 10am–5pm, Sat 11am–6pm.
Donation suggested.
Subway: Eastern Parkway/Brooklyn Museum.

Cobble Hill
A sedate neighbourhood of brownstone houses and red-brick terraces. Jenny Jerome, mother of British prime minister, Sir Winston Churchill, was born at 197 Amity Street.
Subway: Borough Hall.

Coney Island
At one time, Coney Island was the most famous amusement resort in the world. Today, all that remains are more than three miles of beach and lots of typical seaside amusements, all a bit run down.
Subway: Coney Island.

The Esplanade
Better known as 'The Promenade', this narrow strip of parkway overlooks the East River. Visitors contemplate the view of Manhattan as the joggers pound by.
Located at the East River end of Pierrepont St. Subway: Clark St.

Brooklyn Botanic Garden in full bloom

Walk: Brooklyn Heights

Gracious living of the past is still evident from the brownstone houses and opulent avenues of Brooklyn Heights, a 50-block historic district.

Allow 2 hours.

Begin at the Manhattan end of Brooklyn Bridge. Walk across the bridge's wooden promenade. Look out for two floating restaurants moored here. Leave by the left fork, go under the bridge to Cadman Plaza West, following it westwards to Old Fulton St. The route goes under the Brooklyn-Queens Expressway.

1 Old Fulton Street

Although in a rather drab area, Old Fulton Street leads to the part-cobbled Fulton Ferry Landing, from which there is a good view of Manhattan's skyline. It is opposite South Street Seaport, and is named after the steam ferry that Robert Fulton operated to transport Brooklyn's businessmen between home and Wall Street before the bridge started functioning in 1883.

Return along Old Fulton St, turning right at Everit St into Columbia Heights, then left into Middagh St.

2 Middagh Street

Number 24 Middagh Street, at the corner of Willow Street, is the oldest home in the area, a timber-built, highly ornamented 'gingerbread' house dating from the 1820s. (Gingerbread refers to the decorative wooden embellishment to the buildings' exteriors.) Following the custom of the day, Middagh Street was named after a prominent 19th-century family, one of whom so disliked this

practice, that she named several local streets after trees and fruit instead.
Continue along Middagh, turning right at Hicks St and left at Orange St.

3 Orange Street
Plymouth Church of the Pilgrims is where the clergyman Henry Ward Beecher preached passionately for the abolition of slavery, and harboured runaways from the South before the Civil War. A statue of Beecher stands in a courtyard next to the church.
Return across Hicks St, turning left into Willow St.

4 Willow Street
This attractive thoroughfare offers a wide range of architectural styles. Henry Ward Beecher lived at No. 22, a classic-style brownstone. Other houses in the street are in the Queen Anne style, and there is a short row of 17th-century Federal houses that is believed to have been part of the 'underground railroad', a clandestine organisation which helped fugitive slaves.
Turn right on to Pierrepont St and cross Columbia Heights to the Brooklyn Heights Promenade.

5 The Promenade
Also known as The Esplanade, this leads through a narrow park, hanging above the East River, providing the best view of Lower Manhattan.
Continue south along The Promenade, turning left into Montague St.

6 Montague Street
This is a vibrant shopping street with galleries, antiques, bars, book stores, and a wide choice of national cuisines. Some famous writers have lived in the area, including Arthur Miller, Truman Capote, WH Auden, and Thomas Wolfe. Recently restored, the first stained-glass windows made in the USA can be seen at the Church of St Anne and the Holy Trinity at the corner of Montague and Clinton streets.
Turn right into Clinton St and right again into Remsen St.

7 Remsen Street
At No. 113 Remsen Street is the Maronite Cathedral of Our Lady of Lebanon, built in Romanesque revival style, and containing fitments from the SS *Normandie*, wrecked in 1943.
Turn left into Hicks St.

8 Hicks Street
Halfway between Remsen and Joralemon streets is Grace Court Alley, which contains a couple of dozen dignified mews homes. Further on Hicks Street is Grace Church, designed in Gothic Revival style in the mid-1990s by the architect Richard Upjohn.
Continue south along Hicks St, cross State St, and turn left into Atlantic Ave.

9 Atlantic Avenue
Lebanese, Syrian, and Yemeni eateries and food stores form a Middle Eastern quarter between Hicks and Court streets. The air is rich with the scents of mingled spices and baking pastries. The area is also known for its antique shops.
Turn left into Court St. Continue to Joralemon St, where the return journey to Manhattan can be made from Borough Hall subway station.

Brooklyn Lifestyle

There was a time when Manhattanites, if they thought about it at all, regarded Brooklyn as no more than an urban dormitory on the opposite shore of the East River. Not any more. Brooklyn has come to be recognised for what it has, in fact, always been: a lively community with an identity uniquely its own, some handsome and highly desirable residential areas, and a vibrant mix of ethnic and cultural heritages.

Until 1898, when, after the opening of the Brooklyn Bridge spanning the East River, it was annexed into Metropolitan New York, Brooklyn was a city in its own right, covering 77 square miles, and composed of six main towns and a number of small villages. If it were still independent, it would be the third largest city in the USA. It has a population double that of Manhattan.

Its neighbourhoods have managed to retain their individuality. Brooklyn Heights, the historic district with its very pretty streets, has a clear identity – a little snooty, perhaps, here and there – but you have only to move a few blocks to find something totally different. At Cobble Hill, for instance, bits of the

Yemen, Syria, and Lebanon have been dumped along a stretch of Atlantic Avenue – a Middle East bazaar of restaurants serving kebabs, hummus, couscous, and the like, and shops rich with the scent of spices, roasting coffee, and baking bread. Further along the ethnic spectrum – and crossing Atlantic Avenue three or four blocks south of Borough Hall – Court Street reflects the lifestyles of Italy and Spain, with stores selling olives and olive oil, fresh pasta, cheeses, and salt cod.

Left: homes from a more gracious age in tree-lined Brooklyn Heights
Right: soaring elegance in Brooklyn Heights
Below: the traditional New York deli

Fulton Ferry Landing

Commuter ferries from Manhattan docked here before Brooklyn Bridge was built. There are plans to restore the area, turning surrounding warehouses into a museum and shopping mall. Great views of the bridge and Lower Manhattan, especially from eateries in Restaurant Row.
At the foot of Old Fulton St, reached by way of Cadman Plaza West.
Subway: High St/Brooklyn Bridge.

Grand Army Plaza

A dramatic circular open space at the entrance of Prospect Park (*see opposite page*), from which radiate Eastern Parkway, Prospect Park West, and Vanderbilt and Flatbush avenues. The Soldiers' and Sailors' Memorial Arch is modelled on the Arc de Triomphe in Paris, and honours the Union forces who were victors in the Civil War. The arch is topped by a dramatic sculpture of a chariot drawn by four horses, and inside are reliefs of presidents Abraham Lincoln and Ulysses S Grant.
Subway: Grand Army Plaza.

Greenwood Cemetery

More entertaining than might be imagined, this huge cemetery contains many elaborate tombs, and makes an interesting place to walk.
500 W 25th St/5th Ave.
Tel: (718) 768 7300. Subway: 25th St.

Harbor Defense Museum

A collection of coastal armaments, uniforms, and equipment going back to the 18th century.
Fort Hamilton, at the Brooklyn end of Verrazano-Narrows Bridge.

Tel: (718) 630 4349. Open: Mon–Fri 1–4pm; first Sat of month, Oct–Jun noon–4pm. Free admission.
Subway: 95th St/Fort Hamilton.

Lefferts Homestead

A Dutch Colonial farmhouse, built in 1776 and now housing a museum, the homestead is inside Prospect Park (*see opposite page*). It features period furniture and there is a programme of temporary exhibitions.
Flatbush Ave/Empire Blvd, Prospect Park. Tel: (718) 965 6505. Open: Apr–Nov, Sat & Sun, 1–5pm; Nov–Dec, Sat & Sun 1–4.30pm. Free admission.
Subway: Prospect Park.

New York Aquarium for Wildlife Conservation

A large collection of rare and colourful fish, whales, seals, and penguins. Dolphins, sea lions, and electric eels perform for the public's entertainment.
W 8th St/Surf Ave, Coney Island.
Tel: (718) 265 FISH. Open: daily 10am–5pm, weekends & summer holidays 10am–5.45pm. Admission charge.
Subway: New York Aquarium.

New York City Transit Museum

Set in a disused 1930s subway station, the museum features 80 years of transit memorabilia from the great age of public transportation. It is scheduled to reopen in 2003 after being renovated.
Boerum Place/Schermerhorn St, Brooklyn Heights. Tel: (718) 243 8601; www.mba.nyc.ny.us/museum Open: Tue–Fri 10am–4pm, Sat & Sun noon–5pm. Admission charge.
Subway: Borough Hall.

Plymouth Church of the Pilgrims

A large, simple church built in the 19th century, this was where the preacher Henry Ward Beecher led his campaign against slavery before the Civil War. The church was a mainline station on the 'underground railroad' that smuggled slaves to freedom. A great campaigning orator, Beecher brought many influential and famous worshippers to the church, including Mark Twain and Abraham Lincoln.
Orange & Hicks sts. Tel: (718) 624 4743; www.plymouthchurch.org Tours are available following the Sun noon service or by appointment. Subway: Clark St.

Prospect Park

Landscaped by the same team that designed Central Park, Olmstead, and Vaux, the park covers 526 acres within which can be found a zoo, music grove, boating lakes, and a skating rink. The Friends of Prospect Park is a group of nature lovers committed to caring for the trees in the park.
Its main entrance is from Grand Army Plaza. Tel: (718) 965 8951; www.prospectpark.org Subway: Grand Army Plaza.

Sheepshead Bay

An inlet marking the end of Brooklyn and the start of Coney Island, the bay is a busy deep sea fishing centre, with boats available for charter on piers along Emmons Avenue. The avenue is a lively place by day or night, with waterside bars and restaurants.
Subway: Sheepshead Bay.

A breath of sea air at Sheepshead Bay

what to see

Long Island

Commuter traffic jams aside, no part of Long Island is much more than two hours by car from Manhattan, yet the island's 120-mile length is rich in diversity: sandy beaches, rich farmland, and historic towns.

Pumpkins for sale at a farm shop in Long Island

African-American Museum
Exhibits display the history, cultural heritage, and contributions of African-American Long Islanders, including special displays from the Smithsonian Institution and Brooklyn Museum.
110 N Franklin St, Hempstead, south of Garden City. Tel: (516) 572 0730. Open: Wed 6–9pm, Thu–Sat 10am–4.45pm. Free admission.

Cold Spring Harbor Whaling Museum
Nineteenth-century whaling exhibits, including 400 pieces of scrimshaw (whalebone carvings). Film and diorama.
Main St, North Shore. Tel: (516) 367

3418. Open: Tue–Sun 11am–5pm. Closed: holidays. Admission charge.

Cradle of Aviation
Air and space museum with vintage aircraft, space exploration vehicles, and aviation memorabilia.
Mitchel Field, Garden City, adjacent to Nassau Community College. Tel: (516) 572 0410; www.cradleofaviation.org

Garvies Point Museum and Preserve
Archaeology and geology exhibits of coastal New York State. Nature trails.
Barry Drive, Glen Cove, Western North Shore. Tel: (516) 671 0300. Open: Wed–Sat 10am–4pm, Sun 1–4pm. Closed: winter holidays. Admission charge.

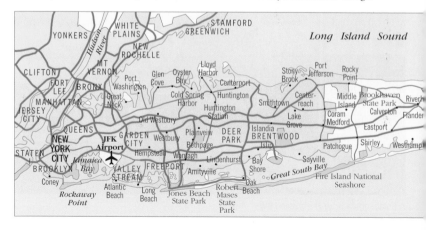

Old Bethpage Lillage Restoration

Pre-Civil War farm village, with inn,
store, church, animals, and costumed
guides. Craft demonstrations.
*Round Swamp Rd, Old Bethpage, east
central Long Island. Tel: (516) 572 8400.
Open: Wed–Sun 10am–5pm. Closed: Jan,
Feb, & holidays, except Memorial Day,
4 July, Labor & Columbus Days, when
closed the day after. Admission charge.*

Raynham Hall

The British headquarters during the
Revolution, the 'saltbox' main house
dates from 1705, and the Gothic wing
from 1851. The 22 rooms contain
period furnishings; formal gardens have
been laid out.
*20 W Main St, Oyster Bay, Eastern North
Shore. Tel: (516) 922 6808;
email: raynham@sinpak.com
Open: Tue–Sun 1–5pm.
Closed: holidays. Admission charge.*

Sagamore Hill National Historic Site

Teddy Roosevelt's retreat for over 30
years, now a National Historical Site, has
been restored in the style of 1901–1909,
the period of his presidency.
*20 Sagamore Hill Rd, Oyster Bay, Eastern
North Shore. Tel: (516) 922 4447.
Open: 1 Jun–10 Sep, daily 9.30am–4pm;
10 Sep–30 May, Wed–Sat 9.30am–4pm.
Closed: Thanksgiving, Christmas Day, &
New Year's Day. Admission charge.*

Sands Point Park and Preserve

The 'Gold Coast' estate of Daniel and
Harry Guggenheim, with Tudor-style
Hempstead House and Castlegould,
influenced by an Irish castle, and Falaise,
a manor house in Norman style. A
nature centre provides information on
the estate's wildlife and trails.
*Middleneck Rd, Port Washington,
North Shore. Tel: (516) 571 7900.
Open: Tue–Sun 10am–5pm.
Admission charge.*

Town Marine Museum

Exhibits on whaling, fishing, and
underwater archaeology, plus model
boats and features on shipwrecks.
*Bluff Rd, off Route 27, between East
Hampton and Amagansett, South Fork.
Open: Jun, weekends 10am–5pm;
Jul–Aug, daily 10am–5pm.
Admission charge.*

Walt Whitman House

The poet Walt Whitman was born here
in 1816. The house is also Long Island's
only New York State Historic Site.
Exhibits, library, shop, and picnicking.
*246 Old Walt Whitman Rd, Huntington,
North Shore. Tel: (516) 427 5240.
Open: Wed–Fri 1–4pm, Sat–Sun
10am–4pm. Closed: holidays.
Free admission.*

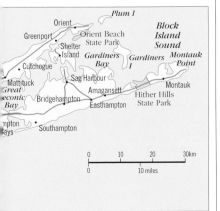

Queens

Most visitors to New York City see Queens before any of the other boroughs, as both John F Kennedy and LaGuardia Airports are in Queens. This is New York's biggest borough, and has the second largest population – nearly two million, including neighbourhoods of Italian, Middle Eastern, Asian, Jewish, Hispanic, Greek, and African Americans.

Signpost to one of the city's elegant old homes

The world spotlight is on Queens when the US Open Tennis Championships take place at Flushing Meadow Park, site of the World Fairs of 1939 and 1964. Queens is also home to the New York Mets baseball team, and two of USA's most prestigious thorough-bred race-tracks, the Aqueduct and Belmont Park.

Whereas many of New York City's residential areas evolved naturally in an era of rapid growth, Queens has seven thoughtfully planned neighbourhoods in which developers allowed for good landscaping and recreational facilities. These neighbourhoods, founded on the garden city concept, have been dubbed the Seven Sisters, the best known being a mock Tudor-style township called Forest Hills Gardens.

Though intended as a low-cost housing project, gentrification elbowed its way in almost before it began, and the well-off – including a strong Jewish community – moved in. Forest Hills is the home of West Side Tennis Club, where the US Open used to be held.

Probably the prettiest of the Sisters is Kew Gardens, with tree-lined streets of well-kept houses in a range of styles. Like Forest Hills, Sunnyside Gardens, in Long Island City, was meant for the working classes when it rose from a swamp in the 1920s. But most lost their homes in the 1930s slump.

Jackson Heights, home of many South Americans, Douglaston, Richmond Hill, and the sublimely named Fresh Meadows are the other Sisters.

The American Museum of the Moving Image

Dedicated to film, television, and video, the museum, opened in 1988, gives an insight into production, and has a permanent exhibition on the development of the art form in addition to thousands of items of film memorabilia. Original sets, and costumes worn by the stars, are displayed, and temporary exhibitions held. Before Hollywood, Astoria was the beating heart of the American movie business, and is now making a comeback (*see p148*). The museum is adjacent to the Kaufman Astoria Studios.

35th Ave/36th St, Astoria.
Tel: (718) 784 0077; www.ammi.org
Open: Tue–Fri noon–5pm, Sat–Sun 11am–6pm. Admission charge.
Subway: Steinway St.

Aqueduct Race Track

This is the largest thoroughbred track in the country, and the only one with its own subway station.

Rockaway Blvd/108th St, Ozone Park. Tel: (718) 641 4700. Open: Oct–May. Closed: Tue. Gates open 11am, first race 1pm. Subway: Aqueduct Race Track.

Belmont Park Race Track

Home of the 'third jewel' in the Triple Crown of thoroughbred racing, the Belmont Stakes – the others are the Kentucky Derby and Preakness. Beautiful grounds with picnic areas and trackside restaurant.

Hempstead Turnpike, Belmont, Long Island. Tel: (516) 488 6000. Open: May–Jul & late Aug. Closed: Tue.

Rail: Long Island railroad from Manhattan's Penn Station to Queens Village.

Bowne House

One of the city's oldest houses, built in 1661, now a museum illustrating how Quaker John Bowne successfully led the struggle for religious freedom in the 17th century when the Quakers were banned under Dutch rule. Generations of Bownes lived at the house until 1947, and their furnishings and ornaments are well displayed.

37–01 Bowne St, Flushing. Tel: (718) 359 0528. Open: Tue, Sat, & Sun 2.30–4.30pm. Special tour by appointment. Admission charge. Subway: Main St.

The delightful exterior of John Bowne's house

Flushing Meadows-Corona Park

Site of the 1939 and 1964 New York
World Fairs, the park is dominated by
the Unisphere, a massive steel globe, and
offers boating and a marina, a
swimming pool, indoor ice skating,
cycling, pitch and putt, a carousel,
theatres, the Queens Zoo (see p123), a
children's farm zoo, and the Queens
Museum (see p122). The park is home to
the National Tennis Center where the
annual US Open is held.
*Jewel/Roosevelt aves, Flushing. Tel: (718)
760 6565. Subway: Shea Stadium.*

Friends' Quaker Meeting House

Built in 1694, it is the borough's oldest
place of worship, and is still used.
*137–16 Northern Blvd, Flushing.
Tel: (718) 358 9636.
Open: 11am–1pm every Sun.*

Isamu Noguchi Museum

Works by the Japanese sculptor, who
died in 1988, in the museum and
adjoining sculpture garden.
*32–37 Vernon Blvd, Astoria.
Tel: (718) 204 7088. Open: Apr–Nov,
Wed, Sat, & Sun 11am–6pm. Hourly
buses leave Asia Society, Park Ave/70th St,
Manhattan, at 30 minutes past the hour,
11.30am–3.30pm.
Admission charge.*

Jamaica Arts Center

This is a multi-ethnic performing and
visual arts centre in an 1898 Italian
Renaissance revival building.
*161–04 Jamaica Ave. Tel: (718) 658 7400.
Open: Mon–Fri 9am–8pm, Sat
9am–7.30pm. Free admission.
Subway: Jamaica Center
(Parsons/Archer).*

Flushing Meadows, known worldwide for the US Open tennis matches held here

Jamaica Bay Wildlife Refuge (Gateway National Recreation Area)

Almost as big as Manhattan in area, the refuge is reserved for nature walks and has 300 species of birds. Visitor permit available in grounds.
Crossbay Blvd, Broad Channel.
Tel: (718) 318 4340.
Open: daily dawn–dusk.
Free admission. Subway: Rockaways.

Kingsland Homestead (Queens Historical Society)

Colonial farmhouse built in 1774. Exhibits relating to its history are displayed. The historical society, which provides a do-it-yourself tour leaflet, is headquartered in the house. Outside is a weeping beech tree planted as a cutting from Belgium in 1847, and now officially an historical landmark.
143–35 37th Ave, Flushing.
Tel: (718) 939 0647.
Open: Tue, Sat, & Sun 2.30–4.30pm.
Admission charge. Subway: Main St.

LaGuardia Community College Archives

Interesting for its collection of papers of popular New York City Mayor Fiorello LaGuardia, elected in 1933 during the Depression.
31–10 Thomson Ave. Tel: (718) 482 5421.
Open: Mon–Fri 9am–9.45pm, Sat 9am–5pm. Subway: 33rd St.

New York Hall of Science

Science and technology exhibits include *Seeing the Light*, *Realm of the Atom*, *Hidden Kingdoms*, and the *World of Microbes* – topics appealing to children as well as adults. Lots of hands-on

exhibits for children.
47–01 111th St, Flushing Meadows.
Tel: (718) 699 0005; www.nyhalsci.org
Open: Mon & Tue 9.30am–2pm (groups only), Wed–Sun 9.30am–5pm. Admission charge. Subway: Shea Stadium.

New York State Supreme Court House

Opposite the tall Citicorp Building, this is often used for the shooting of courtroom drama movies, as well as real-life trials.
25–10 Court House Square.
Subway: 45th St/Court House Square.

PS1 (Project Studio 1)

Cultural centre converted in 1976 from a 19th-century school building, combining art gallery and artists' studios, with occasional exhibitions.
22–25 Jakson Ave at 46th Ave.
Long Island City. Tel: (718) 784 2084;
www.ps1.org Open: Wed–Sun noon–6pm. Admission charge.

Queensborough Bridge

Opened in 1909, this 7,000-foot long bridge across the East River is worth a look. There is a riverside park at the bridge's base.

Method in the Madness

After you have conquered Manhattan's no-nonsense way of numbering its streets and avenues – which does not take long – you come down to earth with a bump when you start exploring Queens. There may be method in the system. If so, it eludes many visitors. If nobody can explain to you how to get to a particular attraction or restaurant, telephone your destination, stating where you are, and ask for exact directions.

There are fascinating exhibits for the young at the New York Hall of Sciences

Queens Botanical Garden

Seasonal floral displays on a 39-acre site. The senses are charmed by herb, bee, bird, and rose gardens; crab-apple trees and Japanese cherry groves; and a Victorian wedding garden. There is also plant and gift shop.

43–50 Main St, Flushing. Tel: (718) 886 3800. Open: Tue–Sun 10am–6pm, 8am–7pm in summer. Closed: Mon except for school groups. Free admission. Subway: Main St.

Queens County Farm Museum

This restored 200-year-old working farm traces the agricultural history of New York City. Outdoor weekend events in spring, summer, and autumn.

73–50 Little Neck Parkway, Floral Park. Tel: (718) 347 FARM. Open: weekdays 9am–5pm; Apr–Dec weekends, noon–5pm. Free admission.

Queens Museum

A popular exhibit is the enormous Panorama, a continually updated illuminated model of the five boroughs of New York City, a useful aid to getting your bearings and spotting what you want to see in the full-size version.

Exhibits keep changing. The museum building was the New York Pavilion during the 1939 New York World Fair.

NYC Building, Flushing Meadows. Tel: (718) 592 9700. Open: Wed–Fri 10am–5pm, Sat & Sun noon–5pm, Tue for groups by appointment. Closed: Mon. Admission charge (children under 5 yrs free). Subway: Shea Stadium.

Queens Zoo

Recently refurbished zoo at west side of Flushing Meadows-Corona Park, with North American animals in their natural habitats.

Jewel/Roosevelt aves, Flushing. Tel: (718) 271 7761. Open: 10am–5pm weekdays, weekends & holidays 10am–5.30pm. Admission charge. Subway: Shea Stadium.

The Rockaways

Nearly 10 miles of beaches on a spit of land in the Atlantic Ocean, with Jacob Riis Park at the western end. Take the subway to Rockaway Park Beach, or to stops at several beaches northwards.

St Demetrius Cathedral

The cathedral has the biggest Orthodox congregation outside Greece.
30–11 30th Drive, Astoria.
Subway: Broadway.

Shea Stadium

Home of the New York Mets baseball team, it seats 55,000.
126th St/Roosevelt Ave, Flushing Meadows-Corona Park. Tel: (718) 507 8499. Subway: Shea Stadium.

Socrates Sculpture Park

Larger-than-life sculptures, some abstracts, in a four-acre riverfront setting opposite the Isamu Noguchi Museum (*see p120*).
31–29 Vernon Blvd, Astoria.
Tel: (718) 956 1819.
Open: summer, daily 10am–dusk; winter, weekends.
Donation suggested.

Around Queens

Long Island City is an industrial and commercial area of Queens; there used to be a good ferry connection with Manhattan. Development began early in the 19th century. Prosperous business people built gracious homes along the frontage of the East River in Vernon Boulevard. Huntspoint Historic District, 45th Avenue, provides a pleasant stroll among well-maintained rowhouses with quaint verandas. Around a small park at 21st Street are warehouses providing studio space for artists at much lower rents than those demanded on Manhattan.

There is a palpable air of suspense at the Shea Stadium

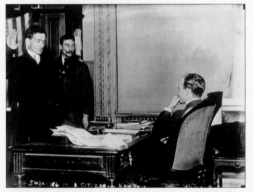

In 1626, the governor, Peter Minuit, stood at Old Fort Amsterdam – later to become the site of the US Customs House at Bowling Green – to acquire Manhattan Island from a party of Algonquin Indians for $24-worth of baubles, beads, and brightly coloured cloth. Governor Minuit reckoned he had a great bargain, and since it was not theirs to sell, the Algonquins, too, were happy with the arrangement.

Once upon a time, the tallest building in New York was a two-storey windmill. That was in 1664 when Dutch rule of the place, then called Nieuw Amsterdam, was drawing to a close. In 1624, thirty families had sailed from Holland to settle on Nut Island – now known as Governor's Island – in New York Harbor. The settlement grew rapidly.

A year earlier, in 1625, the Dutch had formed the fur trading post of Nieuw Amsterdam. Beaver fur was the mainstay of the enterprise, and the beaver still features in the city's seal. The Dutch built a wall from the East River to the Hudson River in 1653 – Wall Street

follows its line – to protect their colony from Indians, and from British trade competitors.

But in 1664, the British took the city without a fight (Dutch Governor Peter Stuyvesant reluctantly surrendered the city), and named it after the Duke of York, the brother of King Charles II. Lower Manhattan was like a ping-pong ball for a time. The Dutch recaptured it in 1673, calling it New Orange, and the British regained control the following year, remaining in charge until the

Revolutionary War ended in 1783, with the Americans gaining independence. George Washington was sworn in as the first president at Federal Hall in New York.

Facing page above: Swearing in a new US citizen; below: Peter Minuit buys Manhattan for $24-worth of trinkets
Above: The Dutch arrive on Staten Island; below: New York in 1673

Staten Island

Until the Verrazano-Narrows Bridge opened in 1964,
linking it with Brooklyn, Staten Island was the poor
relation of New York City. It was a small fishing and
farming community which tended to keep itself to itself.
Once the bridge went up, neighbours looked covetously at
the property prices in Staten Island, bought land, set up
desirable residences, and commuted. Nevertheless, enough
of the rural greenery and woodland has been retained to
put the smallest borough on the tourist trail, though few
penetrate the interior.

Staten Island may be the least visited of
the city's boroughs, but for those
seeking quiet refuge or sights off the
beaten track it is certainly worth a visit.

Staten Island has a zoo, a restoration
project, a botanical garden, a cultural
centre, and a handful of museums – all
worthy attractions. Most visitors,
however, are attracted by the idea of a
good view of New York Harbor, Ellis
Island, and the Statue of Liberty, which
they can get at no extra charge on the
Staten Island Ferry. They disembark at
Bay Street Landing in the town of St
George.

Those interested in history will find
time well spent on Staten Island. The
attractions are somewhat spread out,
but bus rides to most areas provide an
opportunity to enjoy the scenery. After a
few days in Manhattan, where, at best,
gulls and pigeons represent the wildlife,
non-city dwellers will be relieved to find
rural surroundings. Sports facilities
include golf, hiking, tennis, and – in
winter – skiing and sledging.

Alice Austen House Museum and Garden

Less than two miles south of Bay Street
Landing is the Dutch-style Victorian
cottage overlooking New York Harbor
where the renowned photographer Alice
Austen spent most of her life. She was
given her first camera at the age of 10.
The pictures she took until her death in
her mid-80s in 1952 provide a wonderful
record of Staten Island and its people. A
selection is on view at the restored
cottage. House tours and 'Alice's World'
videos are available. There is a gift shop.
2 Hylan Blvd. Tel: (718) 816 4506.
Open: Thu–Sun noon–5pm.
Bus: S51 from Bay St.

Barrett Park and Cloves Lake Park

Visitors will find a bridle path, ice
skating rink, model boating pond, and
fishing facilities, together with the Staten
Island Zoo, all about one mile southwest
of Snug Harbor.
1150 Clove Rd, West Brighton.
Tel: (718) 390 8000.

Clay Pit Ponds Park
This is the only state park on the island. Horses can be hired from V & S Stables.
83 Nielson Ave, Staten Island.
Tel: (718) 967 1976.

Conference House
A meeting took place here in 1776 with the specific aim of preventing the Revolution. Benjamin Franklin met with John Adams, Edward Rutledge, and the British Admiral Lord Howe, but, as history records, the meeting failed. The stone manor house was built in 1675.
Hylan Blvd, Tottenville, far southwest of the island. Tel: (718) 984 2086.
Open: Mar–Dec, Wed–Sun 1–4pm.
Admission charge.

Council on the Arts and Humanities for Staten Island
This organisation promotes all aspects of the island's diverse cultural life –

A joy ride for many . . .

music, theatre, dance, art, and the humanities. It issues a free guide to cultural events and runs a tourist and cultural information centre across the water in the South Ferry Passenger Terminal, Manhattan.
Snug Harbor Cultural Center, 1000 Richmond Terrace. Tel: (718) 447 3329; email: info@statenislandarts.org
Open: Mon–Fri 9am–5pm.

. . . and a short, but informative luxury cruise for some

Historic Richmondtown regularly recreates Staten Island's past

Garibaldi-Meucci Museum

Who invented the telephone? Antonio Meucci's claim to have done so before Alexander Graham Bell is well documented at this museum, which has mid-19th-century memorabilia and letters and photographs illustrating the life of Italian revolutionary Giuseppe Garibaldi, who spent some time in the borough. The museum is in a restored Federal farmhouse.

420 Tompkins Ave, Rosebank.
Tel: (718) 442 1608. Open: Tue–Sun 1–5pm. Free admission.

Gateway National Recreation Area

Beaches and shoreland at the east of the island, extending over 26,000 acres, with occasional special events. Sports facilities include tennis, volleyball, basketball, baseball, soccer, and football. Managed by the National Parks Service.

Great Kills Park, New Dorp.
Tel: (718) 351 6970. Free admission.

The Green Belt

A 2,500-acre expanse of swamp and freshwater ponds formed by an Ice Age glacier, with woodlands, grassland, and wetlands, and trails to follow. Animals and birds in their natural habitats. High Rock Park Conservation Center, a popular hiking area, is within the Green Belt. Amenities include a visitor centre, gallery, and gift shop. Guided and self-guided tours are available.

200 Nevada Ave/Rockland Ave.
Tel: (718) 667 2165. Open: Mon–Fri 9am–5pm. Free admission.

Jacques Marchais Center of Tibetan Art

A reproduced Buddhist monastery, situated on a steep hillside, housing the

western hemisphere's biggest collection of Tibetan art works, musical instruments, ornaments, costumes, bronze images, and ritual objects. Educational programmes are on offer. Phone for the date of the Harvest Festival celebrated by monks at the Center in the first half of October, when Tibetan foods and craft works are on sale. Jacques Marchais was an arts dealer.
338 Lighthouse Ave, Staten Island. Tel: (718) 987 3478. Open: mid-Apr–mid-Nov, Wed–Sun 1–5pm; Dec–Mar by appointment only. Admission charge. Bus: 115 from ferry terminal.

Museum of the Staten Island Institute of Arts and Sciences

About one mile east of Snug Harbor, the museum has displays of natural history and fine arts.
75 Stuyvesant Place, St George. Tel: (718) 727 1135. Open: Mon–Sat 9am–5pm, Sun 1–5pm. Donation suggested.

Richmondtown Restoration

Founded in the late 17th century,

Richmondtown was the county seat of the island, and is now Staten Island Historical Society's ongoing labour of love. There are 26 historic buildings on a site of nearly 100 acres. Some of the buildings have been brought from elsewhere on Staten Island and reconstructed, blending in with the original 18th-century buildings. The 1695 Voorlezer's House is the oldest standing elementary school in the USA. There is a general store, plenty of old Dutch colonial architecture, and the 1740 Guyon-Lake Tyson House, on Staten Island's first permanent settlement, dating back to 1685. The visitor centre is housed in the 19th-century Greek Revival courthouse. The historic museum traces 300 years of Staten Island life. Toys, furniture, tools,

A Gift from New York

Staten Islanders are remarkably tolerant of visitors from 'the city' as they call Manhattan, considering that they also receive most of New York's garbage, making the Fresh Kills garbage dump arguably the biggest landfill site in the world.

Not just a place to see, but also a place for discussion on Buddhism

china, and other domestic and agricultural items of past centuries are exhibited, with a vast collection of photographs, including many works of Alice Austen, a local recorder of events and people. The restored village is frequently the scene of special events, including flea markets, an Easter egg hunt, a Yankee Pedlar day, a display of Staten Island samplers, an antique and craft market, a Civil War encampment weekend, and an Independence Day ice-cream social. Craftspeople and tradespeople in costume use the techniques of long ago. The village includes a museum of childhood, with antique dolls and toys and small-scale furniture.

441 Clarke Ave at Arthur Kill/Amboy rds. Tel: (718) 351 1611. Open: Jan–Mar, Wed–Fri 1–5pm; Apr–Jun & Sep–Dec, 1–5pm; Jul & Aug, Wed–Fri 10am–5pm, Sat & Sun 1–5pm. Admission charge. Bus: S74 Richmond Road from ferry terminal.

Snug Harbor Cultural Center

National Historic District of American Architecture on 83 acres of parkland. Originally a farm overlooking a waterway that runs into Upper New York Bay, it became a 'snug harbor' for retired sailors in 1831.

There are several Greek Revival temple-like buildings with columns, one of which still reflects its nautical connections in the pictures and ornaments in its main hall. Today, there are displays of contemporary art and sculpture, and musical performances and indoor concerts are held in the Veterans' Memorial Hall, the former

chapel. Outdoor concerts and recitals are given in summer by such high-calibre players as the New York Philharmonic and the Metropolitan Opera. Guided tours of the centre are given on weekend afternoons.

1000 Richmond Terrace. Tel: (718) 448 2500. Open: daily 8am–dusk. Charge for group tours. Trolley service between ferry terminal and Snug Harbor, or S40 bus.

Staten Island Children's Museum

An imaginative museum, it has some revolving exhibitions in which children can participate, learning about natural history and aspects of everyday life, such as the television. Exhibitions are held in the grounds in the Newhouse Center for Contemporary Art.

1000 Richmond Terrace/Snug Harbor Rd. Tel: (718) 273 2060. Museum open: Tue–Sun noon–5pm on schooldays, 11am–5pm on holidays. Admission charge. For special programmes and workshops, tel (718) 448 6557. Newhouse Center open: Wed–Sun noon–5pm. Donation suggested.

Staten Island Botanical Garden

On the Snug Harbor complex, the 80-acre site includes a scented garden for the blind, a perennial garden, 10 acres of natural marsh habitat, specimen trees, ponds, a greenhouse, a bonsai collection, and beds of floral displays. On Sunday afternoons you can take a guided tree walk.

1000 Richmond Terrace/Snug Harbor Rd. Tel: (718) 273 8200; www.sibg.org Open: Tue–Sun 10am–5pm. Admission charge.

Staten Island Zoo

Small, with the accent on quality rather than quantity, the zoo is renowned as the home of one of the world's finest reptile collections. A children's zoo is incorporated.
Barrett Park, 614 Broadway.
Tel: (718) 442 3100/3174;
www.statenislandzoo.org
Open: daily 10am–4.45pm.
Admission charge.

Verrazano-Narrows Bridge

Opened in 1964, with twin towers the height of a 70-storey building supporting the 4,260-foot suspension span, this bridge links Staten Island and Brooklyn. It was the world's longest suspension bridge until one was built over the River Humber in the United Kingdom. It was constructed by Othmar Ammann, a man already responsible for overseeing the building of eight other New York bridges. More than 30,000 runners cross it in the New York Marathon.

William T Davis Wildlife Refuge

260 acres of woodland, fields, tidal marsh, and freshwater wetlands. Plants, animals, birds, and reptiles which may be encountered are indicated on the trails. Tours can be arranged.
Travis/Richmond aves, New Springville.
Tel: (718) 667 2165. Open: daily dawn–dusk. Free admission.

Antique Haven

Close to the ferry terminal at Staten Island is St George's, where a number of shops, including a group in the Edgewater Hall Antiques Center, a converted bank building, sell furniture, artefacts, and adornments of days gone by.

Staten Island Children's Museum

Getting Away From It All

Even in New York there comes a time when visitors yearn for a change of pace and scene. It happens to New Yorkers themselves, who are great weekenders. There are many interesting and exciting things to see and do within easy reach, and the choice widens considerably for those who can take a break of two or three days.

Not an obvious choice for a day out, but an interesting one

Open Spaces

New York has no shortage of open space among all those cubic miles of glass and concrete. More than 1,500 parks and playgrounds alone cover a total of 26,000 acres.

Beaches

There are several good beaches close to Manhattan. Most can be reached by subway, but some get very crowded on summer weekends. Quieter coastal areas – with better beaches – are to be found further east on Long Island.

Brooklyn's beaches can all be reached by the subway's D train, so naturally they pull in the crowds. Brighton Beach, at the eastern end of Coney Island (which is actually a peninsula), is in the area known as Little Odessa, because so many of its residents are Russian immigrants.

Coney Island Beach is the archetypal seaside resort, brash and popular, with amusement arcades and fairground rides. Once fashionable, it first attracted attention in the 1840s. In recent years, however, it has declined, although the standard of its traditional ethnic snacks remains high.

Smaller than either of the two above beaches, Manhattan Beach is on the same stretch of Coney Island coast, but is a little more up-market, and mainly attracts local residents.

The best of the beaches close to Manhattan – and therefore the most popular – is **Rockaway Beach**, 7½ miles of sand and surf on a spit of land south of Jamaica Bay. Subway trains A and C stop at stations along the beach. To the west is Jacob Riis Park, which has good sandy beaches, popular with the gay community.

Further east on Long Island, the white sands of Long Beach and Jones Beach State Park entice New Yorkers beyond the Metropolitan boundary. Both can be reached by train from Manhattan's Penn Station to Freeport, where there is a bus connection.

Botanical Gardens

Covering an area of 52 acres, Brooklyn Botanic Garden is an intimate retreat next door to the Brooklyn Museum. Its main feature is an enchanting Japanese Garden, and there are fragrance, rose, and herb gardens, as well as a conservatory with tropical, desert, and temperate pavilions. **New York Botanical Garden** in the Bronx covers

250 acres alongside the Bronx River Gorge. Inspired by London's Kew Gardens, it includes a 40-acre forest among its attractions (*see also pp102–3*). Staten Island Botanical Garden is on 80 acres at Snug Harbor, and features trees, ponds, and a natural marsh habitat (*see also p130*).

Cemeteries

A cemetery might be the last place you would expect to visit on holiday, but two in New York are certainly worth the visit. Both have illustrious and notorious names on elaborate tombs.

At Brooklyn's **Greenwood Cemetery**, you can take a guided tour of its 478 acres. Among its incumbents are members of the Steinway piano family in a 119-room mausoleum. **Woodlawn Cemetery**, North Bronx, is the last resting place for a number of famous names, among them the jazz wizard Duke Ellington.

Coney Island's funfair is popular with families

Parks

Fort Tryon and Inwood Parks, at the northern end of Manhattan, offer stunning views of the Hudson River and New Jersey shore. Landscaped by Frederick Law Olmsted, the Central Park designer, Fort Tryon encompasses **The Cloisters** (*see p46*), which houses the Metropolitan Museum of Art medieval collection. Inwood, where Indian cave dwellers once lived, contains the Dyckman House, a restored 18th-century Dutch farmhouse.

Kissena Park in southwest Flushing, Queens, has walking trails through its 235 acres of protected forest and marshland. **Pelham Bay Park**, on the northeast edge of the Bronx overlooking Long Island Sound, is the city's largest, covering more than 2,000 acres. It was purchased from the Indians by Thomas Pell in 1654, and today lists canoeing, cycling, horse riding, and a mile of beach among its amenities. In Brooklyn, Prospect Park has a zoo, music grove, skating rink, and boating lakes in 526 acres.

River Trips

Manhattan's most obvious open space is the water that surrounds it: a 35-mile trip lasting three hours if the island is circumnavigated. Circle Line offers trips up to 13 times a day from its own plaza at the Hudson River end of 42nd Street. The trips, which run all year round, introduce all five boroughs, and vessels pass many famous landmarks. There is also a two-hour evening cruise of New York Harbor and Lower Manhattan. Metropolitan Cruise Line, Spirit of New York, and World Yacht offer luncheon

Madison Square Park

and dinner cruises around Manhattan. (*See p185 for more information.*)

Wildlife

Central Park after dark and the subway's seedier sections are not the only places to observe life in the wild in New York. Gentler, more natural aspects can be viewed – often unexpectedly – in many locations.

Birdwatchers will have a rewarding time in Central and other parks. Large tracts of seashore, especially on Long Island, offer sanctuary to many varieties of wildfowl and seabirds. Whale-watching tours operate from Montauk, at the eastern tip of Long Island.

Jamaica Bay Wildlife Refuge straddles the southern boundaries of Brooklyn and Queens, and lies beneath the JFK

Airport flightpath. Nevertheless, some 300 species of birds and small mammals manage to live there undisturbed, especially egrets and herons, and an abundance of waders and other shorebirds. Covering more than 9,000 acres of land and water, the refuge is almost as big as Manhattan.

To the east, Jones Beach State Park, Lawrence Marsh, Orient Beach State Park, and Moriches Bay present wonderful opportunities for beachcombers to seek out clams and crabs, shells and sand dollars, shoreline vegetation, and yet more birds. Long Island's rural terrain – pastures and woodland – is the habitat of such species as the blue jay, the colourful American goldfinch, catbirds, and mockingbirds, and for mammals including chipmunks and grey squirrels.

Naturalists will find it worthwhile taking a break in New Jersey. Great Swamp National Wildlife Refuge, a few miles west of Newark, has both marsh and woodland habitats harbouring warblers, flycatchers, woodpeckers, rails, ducks, and herons. Brigantine National Wildlife Refuge, near Atlantic City, has egrets, herons, and ibises in a labyrinth of freshwater pools and saltmarshes. Further south, Cape May is renowned for its autumn migrations of warblers, vireos, and birds of prey.

Companionship and a quiet read at the park

OUTER REACHES

A break from the city of two or three days can bring rich rewards. The eastern extremity of Long Island is not much more than 125 miles from Manhattan, and there is much to be seen in the neighbouring states of Connecticut and New Jersey. New York State's attractions are legion and accessible – even Niagara Falls, on the Canadian border, is barely an hour's flight away.

Long Island

Shaped like a squid on the move, Long Island has rural landscapes and sand-fringed shores that soon leave the gritty metropolis behind.

The island's North Shore is more rugged, with wooded headlands, coves, and cliffs, and the mansions that cause its western section to be known as the Gold Coast. Many of the lavish homes were built in the Roaring 20s. The town of Great Neck is the West Egg of F Scott Fitzgerald's novel, *The Great Gatsby*.

The South Shore is best known for its beaches, Jones Beach, Oak Beach, and Fire Island, favoured by gays. There are few places of note in the west of the island, except perhaps Amityville whose haunted house still broods on a hill in the town.

For a real break, it is best to slog on eastwards, where the island divides into North Fork and South Fork. North Fork is wilder, with fewer tourists. Its few towns have a distinctly New England character. Orient Point has a state park and the ferry connects it to New London, Connecticut.

South Fork is best known for The Hamptons – Westhampton, Hampton Bays, Southampton, Bridgehampton, and Easthampton – a group of small, suave towns with wealthy residents. North of The Hamptons, historic **Sag Harbor** is a former whaling port with a Whalers' Presbyterian Church, a whalers' museum, and graves in the Oakland cemetery. To the east, wind-blown Montauk huddles among the sand dunes.

New York State

Travelling north, it is not long before you reach the beautiful countryside of the Hudson Valley. **Tarrytown**, barely 20 miles

SAG HARBOR WHALING AND HISTORICAL MUSEUM

Main/Garden Sts,
Long Island
Tel: (516) 725 0770.
Open: 15 May–30 Sep,
daily 10am–5pm.
Admission charge.

SUNNYSIDE

West Sunnyside Lane,
Tarrytown.
Tel: (914) 631 820.
Open: Jan–Mar, weekends
10am–5pm; Apr–Dec,
daily 10am–5pm.
Closed: holidays.
Admission charge.

US MILITARY ACADEMY

West Point, NY.
Tel: (914) 938 3507.
Grounds and Military
Museum open: daily
10.30am–4.15pm.
Information Center open:
daily 8.30am–4.15pm.
Closed: Thanksgiving,
Christmas, and New
Year's Day.

from midtown Manhattan, was the village in Washington Irving's *Legend of Sleepy Hollow*. Irving himself lived at nearby Sunnyside, a Dutch farmhouse estate now open to the public and well worth a visit. Also in Tarrytown is Lyndhurst, a Gothic Revival mansion, and Philipsburg Manor and Mill, an authentically restored estate that was built by Dutch settlers in the early 17th century. Also accessible from Tarrytown, in Kykuit, is the Rockefeller Mansion, open to the public.

West of the river, and still a mere 40 miles from Manhattan, is Bear Mountain State Park, with hiking trails and boat rentals. Just north of here is the United States Military Academy at **West Point**, a cradle of American military leaders since 1802. West Point has a visitor information centre, a museum, and lots of boisterous parade activity.

Hudson Valley destinations can be reached by bus, train (commuter service from Grand Central Station), Day Line Ferry services, or by car.
Rockefeller Mansion open: Apr–Nov (tel: (914) 631 3992), daily 10am–3pm. Closed: Tue. Admission charge. Tours of the estate begin at Philipsbury Manor on Route 9 in Sleepy Hollow.

Connecticut

An hour and three-quarters' rail journey from New York's Grand Central Station, by Amtrak or Metro-North, leads to New Haven, Connecticut, home of the Ivy League Yale University. Founded in 1701, Yale now has 11,000 students.

The oldest building on the campus, Connecticut Hall, is a Georgian structure of 1752, now the Department of Philosophy. Other old buildings serve as dormitories and classrooms.

Visitors may wander the campus on their own (maps available from the information office at Phelps Gate, College Street). Guided tours leave the information office twice daily.

Long Island is perfect for a quiet vacation by the sea

Shopping

World-famous for its magnificent department stores, New York is also a discount shopper's delight. Designer-label clothes are offered in the Orchard Street area, in the Lower East Side, at a fraction of big-store prices. It is open on Sundays, but closed on Friday afternoons and Saturdays. For electronic goods at discount prices, try Canal Street and Essex Street downtown. In New York you really can 'shop till you drop'.

New York is a shopper's paradise

Where and What to Buy

Speciality shops, boutiques, and exclusive outlets in malls and atriums make for interesting browsing and buying. Try Pier 17 at South Street Seaport, Rockefeller Center, World Financial Center, and Trump Tower.

New York's many ethnic communities, from East Asia to Western Europe, sell handcrafted gifts and other goods in all five boroughs. The major shopping area is midtown Manhattan.

MIDTOWN MANHATTAN
Antiques
Manhattan Art and Antique Center
More than 100 antiques stores and galleries on three floors.
1050 2nd Ave/56th St.
Tel: (212) 355 4400.
The Showcase
135 antique dealers in a three-storey building.
40 W 25th St between Broadway & Avenue of the Americas.
Tel: (212) 633 6063.

Books
Asia Society Bookstore and Gift Shop
Oriental prints, art books, toys, and jewellery.
1725 Park Ave.
Tel: (212) 288 6400.
Barnes & Noble
Balconies, benches, nooks and crannies – and tens of thousands of books.
105 5th Ave at 18th St.
Tel: (212) 802 0099.
Gotham Bookmart
Literary events are held at this famous store, where authors and dramatists were nurtured by the late proprietor.
41 W 47th St, near 6th Ave.
Tel: (212) 719 4448.

Clothing
Brooks Brothers
A high-class menswear establishment.
346 Madison Ave/44th St.
Tel: (212) 682 8800.
H & M
A great place for bargain hunters. A popular haunt for men's and women's fashion.
640 5th Ave, near 51st St.
Tel: (212) 489 0390.
Gucci
The name says it all.
685 5th Ave.
Tel: (212) 826 2600.

Cameras/Electronics
42nd Street Photo
Negotiable discounts on

goods sold by eager
salesmen.
378 5th Ave, near 35th St.
Tel: (212) 594 6565.
Closed: Fri & Sat.
Willoughby's
High reputation for
service at this store of
massed cameras and
accessories.
138 W 32nd St.
Tel: (212) 564 1600.

Department Stores
Barney's New York
A haven featuring
fragrances, jewellery, and
labels from across the
globe.
660 Madison Ave.
Tel: (212) 826 8900.
Bergdorf Goodman
Genteel atmosphere,
beautiful things.
*754 5th Ave between
57th/58th sts.*
Tel: (212) 753 7300.
Bloomingdales
Busy, bazaar-like feel,
with racks crammed
full and sometimes
great mark-downs on
designer goods.
1000 3rd Ave/59th St.
Tel: (212) 705 2000.
Macy's
The world's largest
department store.
151 W 34th St.
Tel: (212) 695 4400.
Manhattan Mall
Eight floors of

speciality shops and
Stern's – fashions for all,
household goods, gifts,
toys, and a food floor.
100 W 33rd St/6th Ave.
Tel: (212) 465 0500.
Saks Fifth Avenue
Gracious living
personified at this store,
founded in the 1920s.
611 5th Ave/50th St.
Tel: (212) 753 4000.

Gifts
Bath & Body Works
Chain of stores packed
with high-quality, scented
bath products.
7 W 34th St, near 5th Ave.
Tel: (212) 629 6912.
Steuben
Fine crystal made at the
Corning Glass Center in
New York State.
*667 Madison Ave at 61st
St.*
Tel: (212) 752 1441.

Jewellery
Tiffany's
Not everything costs the
earth. Pretty things, at
affordable prices, too.
727 5th Ave/57th St.
Tel: (212) 755 8000.

Records
HMV
This British-based chain
carries a large and
excellent selection of
rock, jazz, and R & B.

*565 W 34th St at Herald
Square.*
Tel: (212) 629 0900.

Toys
F A O Schwartz
The ultimate toy
emporium, with friendly
staff in fancy costume.
767 5th Ave/58th St.
Tel: (212) 644 9400.
The Disney Store
Classic Mickey
memorabilia and more.
711 5th Ave & 55th St.
Tel: (212) 702 0702.

DOWNTOWN
MANHATTAN
Antiques
Howard Kaplan Antiques
*827 Broadway between
12th & 13th sts.*
Tel: (212) 674 1000.
Park Antiques
The shop stocks period
furniture dating back to
the early 1700s.
836 Broadway at 13th St.

Books
Biography Bookshop
An extensive range of
biographies from around
the world.
400 Bleecker at 11th St.
Tel: (212) 807 8655.
St Mark's Bookshop
A variety of books for
serious reading.
31st, 3rd Ave at 9th St.
Tel: (212) 260 7853.

Clothing
Banana Republic
Outfitting for travellers,
including tropical wear.
205 Bleecker St.
Tel: (212) 473 9570.
Barneys New York
Menswear of high repute,
including made to order.
236 W 18th St, near 7th
Ave. Tel: (212) 826 8900.
Abercrombie & Fitch
Casual, inexpensive, and
an all-American appeal.
199 Water St at South
Street Seaport.
Tel: (212) 809 9000.

Gifts
Blue Nile
An uptown boutique for
soaps, shampoos, room
sprays, and candles.
324 Bleecker St, near 7th
Ave. Tel: (646) 336 1118.
Movie Star News
Posters galore in a former
carriage house.
134 W 18th St, near 7th
Ave. Tel: (212) 620 8160.

Records
Bleecker Bob's
Rock, reggae, and punk
golden oldies.
118 W 3rd St at McDougal.
Tel: (212) 475 9677.
Disc-O-Rama
The largest collection of
discounted music.
186 W 4th St.
Tel: (212) 206 8417.

Footlight Records
Old musicals and film
soundtracks.
113 E 12th St, near 3rd
Ave. Tel: (212) 533 1572.
Tower Records
Choose your records,
tapes, videos, and CDs
and marvel at the way-
out customers.
692 Broadway/4th St.
Tel: (212) 505 1500.

Toys
Enchanted Forest
A SoHo experience. Toys
and a craft gallery amid
'magic forest' decor.
85 Mercer St between
Spring/Broome sts.
Tel: (212) 925 6677.
The Scholastic Store
A massive kids' bookstore
with toys, puzzles, and
videos.
557 Broadway, near
Prince St.
Tel: (212) 343 6166.

UPTOWN MANHATTAN
Antiques
Alexander's Antiques
Manhattan arts and
antiques centre.
1050 2nd Ave.
Tel: (212) 935 9386.
Flurian Papp
An upper east side
institution offering fine
European crafts.
962 Madison Ave between
E 75th & 76th sts.

Books
Barnes & Noble
A national chain for
cut-price books.
120 E 86th St near
Lexington Ave.
Tel: (212) 423 9900.
Murder Ink
The great literary
detectives are alive and
doing well here.
2486 Broadway,
near 92nd St.
Tel: (212) 362 8905.

Clothes
Givenchy
Classically elegant wear.
710 Madison Ave at
63rd St.
Tel: (212) 688 4338.
Ann Taylor
Very popular for chic
women's clothing.
2380 Broadway at 87th St.
Tel: (212) 721 3130.
Gap
Several locations.
Fabulous jeans, khakis,
and trendy wear, even for
infants.
2300 Broadway at 33rd St.
Tel: (212) 873 2044.

Gifts
The Metropolitan
Museum of Art Shop
Terrific reproductions of
paintings, jewellery, dish-
and stained-glassware.
1000 5th Ave at 82nd St.
Tel: (212) 570 3894.

Mabel's

A glorious menagerie of gifts, all in animal form.
849 Madison Ave between 70th/71st sts.
Tel: (212) 734 3263.

Records
HMV

Massive stock of discs, tapes, and videos.
Second store at 1280 Lexington Ave/86th St.
Tel: (212) 348 0800.

Gryphon Record Shop

However rare the record, there is a good chance it will be in stock here.
233 W 72nd St, near Broadway.
Tel: (212) 874 1588.

Toys
Zany Brainy

Craft supplies, building kits, child development toys, and software.
112 E 86th St near Lexington.
Tel: (212) 427 6611.

The Children's General Store

This tiny shop has stuffed animals, wind-up toys, costumes, and puzzles priced for every budget.
2473 Broadway at 92nd St. Tel: (212) 628 0004.

WNET Store of Knowledge

This place has build-your-own-robots, board games, and countless other games for kids.
1091 3rd Ave at 64th St.
Tel: (212) 223 0018.

West Side Kids

Purely-for-pleasure toys and learn-without-realising-it toys.
498 Amsterdam Ave/84th St. Tel: (212) 496 7282.

Ethnic Shopping
Back from Guatemala

Beautiful mementoes and colourful gifts.
306 E 6th St.
Tel: (212) 260 7010.

Chinese Porcelain Co

Exquisite gifts and souvenirs.
475 Park Ave.
Tel: (212) 838 7744.

Back from Himalayas Crafts & Tours

Wood- and stone-carved items, textiles, herbs, and incense.
2007 Broadway.
Tel: (212) 787 8500.

Things Japanese

Ceramics, scrolls, and other elegant goods.
127 E 60th St.
Tel: (212) 371 4661.

Tibet West

19 Christopher St.
Tel: (212) 255 3416.

Billboards compete with one another for attention on a busy shopping street

Entertainment

More than anywhere else on earth, New York is entertainment. Ballet, classical music, opera; big-cast musicals, jazz, rock; theatre and film; cabaret, discos, piano bars – it is all here, alive and kicking and, at its best, it is absolutely the best in the world.

Current listings are given in the *NY Times*, *Village Voice*, *Village Times*, *Time Out New York* (*TONY*), and the *New Yorker*. Details on availability of regular and discounted tickets can be had from: Telecharge (*tel: (212) 239 6200*); and Ticketmaster (*tel: (212) 307 4100*). Internet events guides include: *www.nycvisit.com; www.culturefinder.com; www.broadway.org; also see p182.*

BALLET AND DANCE

Dance Theater of Harlem
466 W 152nd St.
Tel: (212) 690 2800.
Subway: 157th St/ Broadway.

Juilliard Dance Theater
60 Lincoln Center Plaza, W 65th St.
Tel: (212) 769 7406.

Isadora Duncan International Center for Dance
91 Claremont Ave.
Tel: (212) 662 4591.

Merce Cunningham Studio
55 Bethune St.
Tel: (212) 255 8240.

CONCERTS AND OPERA

Alice Tully Hall
Intimate, yet seating close to 1,100, with acoustics said to be near-perfect, this is an ideal location for performances by the Lincoln Center Chamber Music Society, and celebrated soloists and concert groups.
Lincoln Center, W 62nd St, Broadway.
Tel: (212) 875 5000.

Amato Opera Theater
Up-and-coming professional performers – musicians and singers – give their all in this downtown location.
319 Bowery.
Tel: (212) 228 8200;
www.amato.org

Avery Fisher Hall
Another Lincoln Center hall, it seats 2,740, and is home of the New York

LUNCHTIME CONCERTS

There are many, usually free, lunchtime performances given at an increasing number of locations throughout the city.

Amongst these the best known are the **Citicorp Center Marketplace** (54th Street/Lexington Avenue) and the **Continental Insurance Atrium** (180 Maiden Lane). Also downtown, **Trinity Church** (Broadway/Wall Street) presents free concerts of mostly classical music on Tuesdays at 12.45pm. Similar events take place at 12.10pm on Mondays and Thursdays in **St Paul's Chapel** (Fulton Street/ Broadway).

The American Ballet Theatre is a balletomane's delight

Philharmonic. During the summer its Mostly Mozart series features performers of international stature.
North side of Main Plaza, Lincoln Center.
Tel: (212) 874 2424.

Bargemusic

A floating location for chamber music and jazz, in the shadow of Brooklyn Bridge.
Fulton Ferry Landing, Brooklyn Heights.
Tel: (718) 624 2083.

Brooklyn Academy of Music

Respected for its musical experimentation, and home of the Brooklyn Philharmonic, the Brooklyn Academy of Music (BAM) has entered into a partnership with the Metropolitan Opera to mount innovative opera productions and commission new works.
30 Lafayette Ave, Brooklyn.
Tel: (718) 636 4100;
www.bam.org

Carnegie Hall

World-famous for more than a century – this was where Paderewski was acclaimed in 1891, Leonard Bernstein in 1943, and the Beatles in 1963. Carnegie Hall is an institution for the whole range of musical experience.
154 W 57th St/7th Ave.
Tel: (212) 247 7800;
www.carnegiehall.org

Grace Rainey Rogers Auditorium

Within the Metropolitan Museum of Art, this auditorium hosts classical music by acclaimed artists.
1000 5th Ave/82nd St.
Tel: (212) 570 3949.

A truly entertaining evening of song and music

GREAT OUTDOORS

During the summer, the city's parks are alive with the sound of music. Even the famous Metropolitan Opera and the ever popular New York Philharmonic go alfresco, and performances are free.

In August, the Out-of-Doors festival takes to the **Lincoln Center Plaza** (*tel: (212) 360 1333*) for events in city parks. (*Tel: (212) 877 2011 for Lincoln Center Out-of-Doors information.*)

Free concerts are also performed on Friday and Saturday evenings in the sculpture garden at the **Museum of Modern Art** (*11 W 53rd St. Tel: (212) 708 9850*).

Saturday evening performances take place on Pier 16 at **South St. Seaport** (*tel: (212) 669 9400*), and across the East River a series of Celebrate Brooklyn concerts is held in **Prospect Park**. (*Tel: (718) 788 0055*). **Central Park** also hosts a festival of music – June through August – at Rumsey Field (*www.summerstage.org*).

Metropolitan Opera

Stunning performances with superstar singers in the most elegant of surroundings at the Lincoln Center. The season runs from September to April.
Lincoln Center.
Tel: (212) 362 6000;
www.metopera.org

New York City Opera

In residence at the Lincoln Center's New York State Theater, the company performs popular musicals (*South Pacific, The Sound of Music*, etc), as well as a range of full-blown operas.
Lincoln Center.
Tel: (212) 870 5570; www.nycopera.com

The elegant façade of the Metropolitan Opera House

JAZZ, BLUES, AND FOLK

Angry Squire
Jazz every night.
Reasonably priced food
and drink. No cover
charge at the bar.
216 7th Ave.
Tel: (212) 242 9066.

Birdland
Live jazz nightly, with big
names appearing at
weekends.
2745 Broadway.
Tel: (212) 749 2228.

Blue Note
Expensive, but good jazz
from top performers.
Cover charge varies
according to star quality.
There is a bar charge.
131 W 3rd St.
Tel: (212) 475 8592.

Bradley's
Greenwich Village bar
where local jazz
musicians gather to hear,
and sometimes play with,
big names. No cover
charge on Mondays and
Tuesdays.
70 University Place.
Tel: (212) 473 9700.

Fat Tuesday's
Big names play every
night in the mirrored
basement, a mecca for
traditional jazz fans. It
frequently houses a
packed crowd.
190 3rd Ave.
Tel: (212) 533 7902.

Folk City
Big-name folk performers
appear here from time to
time. Comedy sessions
at weekends.
130 W 3rd St.
Tel: (212) 254 8449.

Greene Street Café
A split-level location in a
converted SoHo ware-
house. Good jazz but bad
viewing unless you book
a table or balcony seat.
101 Greene St.
Tel: (212) 925 2415.

The Speakeasy
Folk music seven nights a
week in a health-food
hideaway frequented
by musicians.
107 MacDougal St.
Tel: (212) 598 9670.

Sweet Basil
Popular jazz restaurant
on the vibrant Bleecker
Street and Seventh
Avenue intersection in

Jazz in the streets

Greenwich Village. Free music on weekend afternoons.
88 7th Ave.
Tel: (212) 242 1785.

Village Vanguard
The city's oldest jazz venue and still presenting big names.
178 7th Ave.
Tel: (212) 255 4037.

NIGHT CLUBS AND DISCOS

Au Bar
Large and spacious club with a chic clientele and friendly staff.
41 E 58th St.
Tel: (212) 308 9455.

Catch a Rising Star
A showcase club for over 20 years; famous for comedy and music by TV celebrities. New talent also gets a chance.
1487 1st Ave.
Tel: (212) 794 1906.

The Limelight
A former church is the setting for a spectacular disco with state-of-the-art sound and video systems. Huge dance floor and three bars.
660 Avenue of the Americas (6th Ave/ 20th St).
Tel: (212) 807 7850.

The Tunnel
Disco dancing in the unlikely setting of an old railway tunnel, complete with tracks.
220 12th Ave.
Tel: (212) 244 6444.

ROCK

Albuquerque Eats
Loud music with Tex-Mex food. Modestly priced.
1470 1st Ave between 76th/77th sts.
Tel: (212) 734 1600.
Also at 375 3rd Ave/ 27th St.
Tel: (212) 683 6500.

The Bottom Line
Big-name groups draw the crowds – especially from nearby NYU.
15 W 4th St/Broadway.
Tel: (212) 228 6300.

CBGB
The initials mean 'Country, Blue Grass, and Blues', but the sound is pure punk in this sleazy, but still immensely popular location.
315 Bowery/Bleecker St.
Tel: (212) 677 0455.

Hard Rock Café
Deafening music with rock memorabilia and burgers.
221 W 57th St between Broadway/7th Ave.
Tel: (212) 459 9320.

Madison Square Garden
Mega-rock performers perform here.
7th/8th aves at W

A busker gets to work on Fifth Avenue

31st/33rd sts.
Tel: (212) 465 6000.

Pyramid Club
Rock 'n' roll until 4am in this live entertainment club.
101 Ave A, between 6th/7th sts.
Tel: (212) 420 1590.

Radio City Music Hall
Venue for big-occasion mainstream acts.
6th Ave/50th St.
Tel: (212) 247 4777.

Shout!
Classic rock 'n' roll on a huge dance floor. Vintage car seats and display.
124 W 43rd St.
Tel: (212) 869 2088.

FILM AND THEATRE

New Yorkers are enthusiastic film- and theatre-goers, and in both respects they have a wide choice. Broadway is best for the big shows – the lavish musicals – and Off-Broadway for the classics and experimental productions. Theatre, by anybody's standards, is expensive – less so in Off-Broadway playhouses – but discount tickets can be obtained (*see p182 for details*). The *New York Times* and *Village Voice* list what's on.

Theatre buffs can join backstage tours of leading Broadway playhouses. Backstage on Broadway, for instance, provides an opportunity to learn about the Theater District from the professionals – stage managers, actors, directors, and designers – on a conducted 90-minute tour demonstrating how a show is put together.
228 W 47th St.
Tel: (212) 575 8065.

Major Off and Off-Off Broadway Companies

Circle Repertory Theater
Up-and-coming plays.
99 7th Ave/Sheridan Square. Tel: (212) 924 7100.

La Mama Experimental Theater Company
Two theatres and a club with a wide range of avant-garde productions.
74A E 4th St.
Tel: (212) 475 7710.

Steve McGraw's
Broadway hits satirised; also witty cabarets.
158 W 72nd St.
Tel: (212) 595 7400.

Negro Ensemble Company
The black experience dramatised.
155 W 46th St.
Tel: (212) 575 5860.

Pan Asian Repertory Theater
Asian and Asian-American performers appear in new or adapted works.
47 Great Jones/E 3rd St.
Tel: (212) 505 5655.

Playwrights Horizons
A venue for new works.
416 W 42nd St.
Tel: (212) 279 4200.

Public Theater
New and classic plays performed in this complex of five playhouses.
425 Lafayette St/Astor Place. Tel: (212) 598 7150.

Ridiculous Theater Company
Unconventional but firmly established; an original mix of classic and camp.
1 Sheridan Square.
Tel: (212) 691 2271.

ASTORIA RE-RUN

New York was a pioneer in film production when Hollywood was no more than a tract of scrubland on the outskirts of Los Angeles. The industry was firmly established in Astoria, Queens, where Paramount and other major companies were located, with stars like Gloria Swanson and Rudolph Valentino under contract.

In the early 1930s, studios began to be set up in California where the climate was more reliable for outdoor filming, and land prices were cheaper. Astoria is now enjoying a comeback. The new studios, fourth largest in the USA, have produced *The Cotton Club* and *The World According to Garp*.

Royal Court Repertory
Specialising in mystery plays. Comedy and drama also performed.
301 W 55th St. Tel: (212) 956 3500.

CINEMA

Generally, cinema tickets are reasonably priced, and the latest films are released first in New York. The New York Film Festival of international productions takes place in the Lincoln Center's Alice Tully Hall annually at the end of September.

Anthology Film Archives (32–34 2nd Ave, *tel: (212) 505 5181*) and **Biograph** (225 W 57th St, *tel: (212) 582 4582*) specialise in re-runs of movie classics.

The **Museum of Modern Art** (*see p67*) has a film library and two theatres which show classic productions, and the **Museum of the Moving Image** (*see p118*) shows foreign and avant-garde films.

Most of the big cinemas for which New York was once famous have now been converted into multi-screen complexes, with up to six movies showing simultaneously. However, two houses can cope with the giant screen productions: the **Ziegfeld** (141 W 54th St, *tel: (212) 765 7600*), and **Radio City Music Hall** (1260 6th Ave, *tel: (212) 247 4777*), which has a 34-foot-high screen.

The Opera House offers music and theatre to suit every taste

Children

Much of the sightseeing in New York City appeals to children as much as to adults. Everyone enjoys a post-concert tour backstage at Radio City Music Hall, or finding out how the sound effects are made at the NBC.

Fun in Central Park

For youngsters, there are plenty of attractions of special appeal which will also fascinate accompanying grown-ups. The new **Children's Museum of Manhattan** (*see p36*) is full of high-tech

Coney Island's fairground

wonders. The accent is on self-discovery. There are enough hands-on experiences to keep children under 12 happily occupied for hours – among them, painting and other handicrafts, and trying on fancy costumes.

Brooklyn also has a children's museum (*see p108*).

The **Guinness World of Records**, at concourse level in the Empire State Building, intrigues all age groups.

Coney Island, one of the world's most famous seaside resorts – though heavily populated in stifling summer weather – has an amusement park (open weekends only) with roller coaster, rides and games, a boardwalk, an extensive beach, and a popular line in hot dogs from Nathan's. It is worth visiting even in winter, as the **New York Aquarium**, with its thousands of exotic fish, is open all year (*see p114*).

The Children's Zoo in **Central Park**, where the residents are mainly pets and farm animals, also has exciting places to scramble over and through, such as a rabbit hole and Noah's Ark. A newly renovated zoo includes an undercover tropical rainforest, with monkeys, reptiles, and birds, and a Polar Circle, with polar bears and penguins (*see p36*).

Some sort of free entertainment – clowning or conjuring – often goes on in the park, and there is an area where the 'Frisbee rules OK'. On Saturday mornings, model boats are raced on the Conservatory Water, and on summer weekends, storytelling sessions are held by the statue of Hans Christian Andersen. Adventure playgrounds, roller skating and skateboarding, an old-fashioned carousel, puppet shows, and row-boating are among pastimes in the park.

The **Bronx Zoo** has one of the largest animal collections in North America, with a Skyfari cable car and a Bengali Express monorail providing a great view of some habitats (*see p101*). Back in Manhattan, at the **World Financial Center**, make sure the children experience the two-part 'listening sculpture' in the Courtyard, where a whisper in one section is clearly heard across the room in another.

Go to **South Street Seaport**, too, on the East River, with its historic ships open to the public, street performers, and Seaport Experience multimedia show (*see p77*).

The **Staten Island Ferry** is now free for the round trip, and there are three-hour sightseeing cruises around Manhattan Island run by Circle Line at various prices.

Few children can resist a good toy shop. **F A O Schwartz** on Fifth Avenue/58th Street will bowl them over. The staff, in fancy costumes, provide a big welcome, and the stock is awesome and fascinating.

Insects and reptiles, dinosaur bones, and a giant stuffed whale are on show at the **American Museum of Natural History** (*see pp29–30*), and the next best

Animals in their natural habitat, Bronx Zoo

thing to a personal visit to the moon can be arranged at the neighbouring **Rose Planetarium**. These attractions, with an all-enveloping Naturemax screen, are located on Central Park West on 79th and 81st streets.

A collector of toys, dolls, and their accessories, exhibits them at her private home. They can be seen, strictly by appointment, for a small charge at **Aunt Len's Doll and Toy Museum** (6 Hamilton Terrace, 141st St/St Nicholas Ave, *tel: (212) 281 4143*).

Sport and Leisure

SPECTATOR SPORTS

Spectator sports are to New York what gladiatorial contests were to ancient Rome – a comparison which is strengthened by the fact that **Madison Square Garden** (MSG), focal point of the city's sporting scene, is popularly known as the Coliseum.

Not everyone admires the Garden as a building, sprawled as it is on top of Penn Station between 31st and 33rd streets at Seventh Avenue. But excitement runs high inside when a major sports event is staged there.

Hailed as the world's most famous sports, entertainment, and convention complex, MSG seats more than 20,000 spectators. Ice hockey and basketball matches take place from October to April. Major international boxing matches are staged throughout the year, as well as many wrestling contests, cleverly choreographed, which get the shriekers and yellers going.

Book tickets by credit card at the box office (*tel: (212) 465 6000*), or Ticketmaster (*tel: (212) 307 7171*).

American Football

New York has two teams, the Jets and the Giants, both of whom play at Meadowlands. The season starts in August. Credit card bookings can be made by telephoning *(201) 507 8900.*

If you are in New York on the third Sunday in January, you will get caught up – like everyone else in the USA – in the excitement of Superbowl, when the two national finalists meet. Television screening starts long before the match, and when the game starts, you may well find you get more ads than action.

If you are not turned on by American football, avoid bars with big screens, where it monopolises everything. On the other hand, if you are a fan, and you cannot get to the match itself, then you know where to go!

Baseball

Played from April to October, the game lasts up to three hours and has a tremendous following. The New York Yankees play at the **Yankee Stadium** (161st St/River Ave in the Bronx, *tel: (212) 293 6000*), and the New York Mets at **Shea Stadium** (Queens, *tel: (718) 507 8499*). The champion teams of the National League and the American League meet for the final in October.

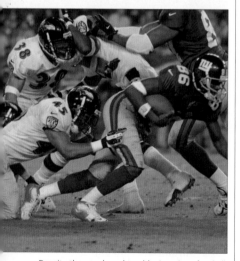

Despite the rough and tumble American football is enjoyed by many

Stadiums are packed to the full for big games

Basketball

The season starts in October, and continues until the championship matches take place in April. The game lasts only an hour, but it is 60 minutes of fast-pace action. New York has two professional teams, the Knicks (short for Knickerbockers), whose home base is Madison Square Garden, and the Mets, who play at Meadowlands.

Horse Racing

Racing enthusiasts have the choice of thoroughbred and harness racing. Both types take place at Meadowlands. Trotting races are between January and August, and flat racing is from September to December.

Harness racing is in the evenings throughout the year at **Yonkers Raceway** (*tel: (914) 968 4200*), just north of the New York City boundary in Yonkers, Westchester County.

The Aqueduct Racetrack in Ozone Park, Queens, is the largest track for thoroughbred racing in the USA. Also in Queens is the **Belmont Park Racetrack**, where the Belmont Stakes, a major race in the American calendar, is run. (*For both, tel: (718) 641 4700.*)

All on-course betting is totalisator. Off-course bets can be placed at one of a number of private OTB (Off-Track Betting) offices. Some are quite grand, with cocktail bars, restaurants, and a small admission charge – and a requirement for men to wear jackets. One of these is the **Inside Track** (*1011 2nd Ave at 53rd/54th sts, tel: (212) 752 1940*). Another is **Skyward** (The Select Club, 165 Water St in the Financial District, *tel: (212) 425 0052*).

New York City Off-Track Betting (*tel: (212) 221 5200*) is America's first government-run off-track betting operation. It has more than 100 branch offices throughout the five boroughs.

Ice Hockey

The New York Rangers' home rink is at Madison Square Garden. The New Jersey Devils play at the Meadowlands Sports Complex across the Hudson River at East Rutherford, New Jersey; and the Islanders at Nassau Coliseum, Uniondale, Long Island.

Tennis

Tickets for the semi-finals and finals of the Open – the US Open Tennis Championships at the **National Tennis Centre** at Flushing Meadow, Queens – do not come cheaply, and those who wish to watch a match need to book well in advance (*tel: (718) 271 5100*).

Grandstand bleacher seating – outdoor uncovered planks (bring an inflatable cushion if your personal upholstery is inadequate) – is on a first-come first-served basis.

The Open takes place in September. In November, the annual Virginia Slims international tournament is held at Madison Square Garden.

PARTICIPATORY SPORTS

Fitness is almost a fetish with many New Yorkers, and for all its temptations in the way of the Inner Man (or Woman) – fast-food joints, hamburger and hot dog stands, happy hours, and Sunday brunches – the city is a surprisingly active place.

Golf

Manhattan is short on space for golf courses, but outside the city limits, on Long Island, there are some of the best courses in the USA, five of them at Bethpage State Park.

Midtown Manhattan has an indoor driving range: the **Richard Metz Golf Studio** (425 Madison Ave/49th St, *tel: (212) 759 6940*).

Horse Riding

The oldest – and now only – riding stable in Manhattan, the **Claremont Riding Academy** (175 W 89th St, *tel: (212) 724 5100*), rents mounts with English-style saddles for riding in Central Park. Western-style saddles are used at **Jamaica Bay Riding Academy** (*tel: (718) 531 8949*) for trail riding in Brooklyn's rural haunts near JFK Airport.

Ice Skating

During the winter months there is ice skating in Central Park, a sport also catered for at several public rinks, where skates can be hired. The **Skyrink** is one (16th floor at 450 W 53rd St, *tel: (212) 239 8385*). It is open all year.

The Central Park location is the Wollman Memorial Rink, in a scenic setting at 64th Street. Small but smart

New York's marathon is a major sporting fixture

and more expensive, but very popular, is the one in the **Rockefeller Center** (*tel: (212) 757 5730*). It opens from 9am to midnight on Fridays and Saturdays, and until 10pm other nights.

Wollman Rink becomes a roller skating rink in summer.

Jogging

Sporty types keen on keeping fit with plenty of exercise always make for **Central Park** where jogging is the obvious (and cheapest) option. Two of the most popular trails in Manhattan are the park's Reservoir Circuit and the East River Promenade.

Joggers flock to the city in their thousands each October to take part in the New York Marathon, a 26-mile course that starts in Staten Island, then sends them streaming across the Verrazano-Narrows Bridge (out of step, hopefully), and through each of the outer boroughs before slumping across the finishing line at the Tavern on the Green in Central Park.

Entry forms: Road Runners Club, PO Box 881, FDR Station, New York, NY 10150. Tel: (212) 860 4455.

Sea Fishing

Boats can be chartered for day or night sea fishing at Sheepshead Bay, in South Brooklyn. The **Jenny Dee** (*tel: (718) 499 4337*) and the **Aviator** (*tel: (718) 769 3108*) take groups of six.

Swimming

New York has several pool and gymnasium complexes. Four locations are: Clarkson Street/7th Avenue (*tel: (212) 397 3147*); 342 E 54th Street (*tel: (212) 397 3148*); 59th Street/West End Avenue (*tel: (212) 397 3120*); and 35 W 134th Street (*tel: (212) 397 3193*).

Tennis

Dozens of courts are maintained by the New York City Parks Department, but the most scenic location is in **Central Park**, where there are 24 courts (near 94th St, *tel: (212) 397 3190*). Daily and summer passes are available. Ambitious players can play where the greats gather – at the USTA **National Tennis Center** at Flushing Meadows, Queens, venue of the US Open. The centre has a number of outdoor and indoor courts available to the public. Those who wish to play must reserve at least two days ahead (*tel: (718) 592 8000*).

Fitness

Sports Center at Chelsea Piers (23rd St at Hudson River, West Side Highway, *tel: (212) 336 6000*) has a rock-climbing wall, a quarter-mile indoor jogging trail, outdoor golf driving range, ice rink, and general fitness centre. **Hackers, Hitters and Hoops** (123 W 18th St, *tel: (212) 929 7482*) is an indoor sports complex. Sightseeing on skates is offered by Stephen Baum's **In-Line Skating Clinics and Tours** (*tel: 800 24 SKATE*). **World Gym** (1926 Broadway, *tel: (212) 874 8942*), has a spacious and well-equipped fitness facility with one-to-one training. Day passes can be purchased.

Vanderbilt YMCA (224 E 47th St, *tel: (212) 756 9600*) has a running track, swimming pool, gymnasium, and exercise classes.

Exercise is a way of life in NY

N ew Yorkers love sports – especially the kinds that exercise the throat and vocal cords, jaw muscles, and drinking elbows. Among men, at least, the major American ball games, plus boxing and hockey (ice hockey, that is, of course) will break down barriers faster than a fireman's axe – and sport is the one subject almost certain to turn the most morose of Yellow Cab drivers into a positive chatterbox.

For most events, essential requirements (for the spectator) are beer (Coke for the juniors), peanuts, and popcorn, which, like hot dogs, can be bought from vendors on the

terraces. It all gets noisy, agitated, and rather messy as the game progresses,

but there is no danger of being the victim of hooligan behaviour. American sports-watching is usually a harmless, if rowdy, pursuit.

Football has the added razzmatazz of marching bands and hyperactive cheerleaders. Baseball-viewing is slightly more sober, possibly because you need to keep your wits about you, as with cricket, to follow what is going on. Horse racing – at Aqueduct Racetrack, Queens, and Belmont Park, Long Island – is as exciting as it is anywhere else in the world, but there is none of the upper-crust picnic ambience associated with European race meetings. Facilities for spectators, however, are excellent, with superb restaurants overlooking the course.

The frantic fever and excitement of American sport reaches a climax during any spectator-sport match

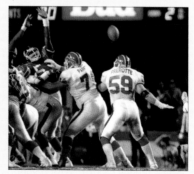

Food and Drink

New York claims to offer the most diverse dining scene in the world. With so many immigrant races having settled in the city over the years, it is not surprising that the cuisine ranges from Afghan to Vietnamese. Eating out has become almost an art form.

For New Yorkers, eating out is a way of life. It is said you could try a different restaurant every night for ten years and not exhaust the possibilities. Inevitably, some close, but new ones open. More than 120 restaurants participate in the annual Summer Restaurant Week where 3-course lunch menus are offered at a fraction of their usual cost.

Price guide for dinner for one person, excluding drink and a tip:

★ inexpensive (under $25)
★★ moderate ($25–$45)
★★★ expensive ($45–$60)
★★★★ very expensive (over $60)

Main specialities to look for on the menu are suggested in some instances, though anyone intent on sampling pickled deer antler and snake wine will have to comb Chinatown or the appropriate location for themselves.

It is worth noting that most Indian restaurants are in the ★ or ★★ category and many serve lunchtime all-you-can-eat buffet meals for around $15.

Some of the more formal restaurants, especially in hotels, demand that men should wear jackets and ties. Reservations are not taken by some establishments.

Check the menu to see if a service charge is imposed.

LOWER MANHATTAN
Bridge Street Cafe ★★
City Hall politicos on both sides like this waterfront café for its seafood and informality.
279 Water St/Dover St. Tel: (212) 227 3344.
Hamburger Harry's ★★
Fat hamburgers broiled over charcoal and

HOME COOKING

Visitors in a suite hotel with a kitchen may like to cook a meal now and again. Vegetables and fruit can be bought at green markets (some open 24 hours a day) or at farmers' markets. **Balducci's** (6th Ave, 9th St, Greenwich Village) stocks 80 varieties of cheese.

For a gourmet food experience, shop at **Zabar's** (2245 Broadway, between 80th and 81st sts), open 365 days a year, up to midnight on Saturday, and always crowded. It has a kitchen-ware department as irresistible as the food – fresh caviar, smoked food, cheeses, and take-out deli. **Burke & Burke**, with a dozen Manhattan branches, provides boxed lunches and picnic packs.

The Amish community sell their produce in the farmers' market at Union Square – lots of pies and pickles, and exquisitely flavoured butters and cheeses (open: Mon, Wed, Fri, & Sat).

applewood, toppings of cheese, caviar, or avocado.
157 Chambers St.
Tel: (212) 267 4446.

Sloppy Louie's ★★
Unpretentious seafood on two floors of former Fulton Ferry Hotel, in Fulton Fish Market.
92 South St.
Tel: (212) 509 9694.

GREENWICH VILLAGE
Caribe ★
West Indian and Spanish cuisine. Try curried goat, conch fritters, and pink margueritas.
117 Perry St/Greenwich St.
Tel: (212) 255 9191.

Gotham Bar & Grill ★★★
Inventive New American cooking.
12 E 12th St,
between 5th Ave &
University Place.
Tel: (212) 620 4020.

La Metairie ★★
The French countryside in New York. Hearty Provençal cuisine.
189 W 10th St/W 4th St.
Tel: (212) 989 0343.

Minetta Tavern ★★
Italian cuisine from noon to midnight.
113 MacDougal St/
Minetta Lane.
Tel: (212) 475 3850.

Wallse ★★★
Big flavours of Viennese cuisine, enough to make

diners waltz.
344 W 11th St.
Tel: (212) 352 2300.

One If By Land, Two If By Sea ★★★
Beef Wellington by candlelight in this 1786 stone carriage house.
17 Barrow St.
Tel: (212) 228 0822.

Whole Wheat 'n' Wildberrys ★
Heaven for vegetarians. Wonderful breads.
57 W 10th St, between
5th/6th aves.
Tel: (212) 677 3410.

TRIBECA
Bouley ★★★★
Considered by many to be the best restaurant in New York. World-class French cuisine in cathedral-like surroundings.
165 Duane St, between
Greenwich/Hudson sts.
Tel: (212) 608 3852.

Chanterelle ★★★★
Innovative French creations in Mercantile Exchange Building. Highly acclaimed.
2 Harrison St/Hudson St.
Tel: (212) 966 6960.

Even speciality restaurants offer great variety

Layla ★★★
Moroccan, Greek, and mid-Eastern flavours mingle while belly dancers gyrate.
211 W Broadway/Franklin St. Tel: (212) 431 0700.

Nobu ★★★
Gastronomic treasures from chef Nobuyuki Matuhisa's kitchen.
1105 Hudson St/Franklin St. Tel: (212) 219 0500.

Rosemarie's ★★
Consistently good value – delicious north Italian cuisine.
145 Duane St, between West Broadway/Church St. Tel: (212) 285 2610.

Thai House Café ★
Possibly the best and cheapest Thai in town.
151 Hudson St/Hubert St. Tel: (212) 334 1085.

SOHO
Ahnell ★★
Enjoy watching beautiful people – and eating Italian food.
177 Prince St, between Thompson/Sullivan sts. Tel: (212) 254 1260.

Aqua Grill ★★★
Fresh fare to fill plates and appetites.
210 Spring St/Ave of the Americas. Tel: (212) 274 0505.

Bell Café ★
Wholesome vegetarian food, pleasantly served. Lively music.
310 Spring St, between Greenwich/Hudson sts. Tel: (212) 334 BELL.

The Cupping Room ★
Renowned for breakfast and brunch. Weekend jazz.
359 West Broadway/ Broome St. Tel: (212) 925 2898.

Elephant and Castle ★
Reliable for a good square meal – burgers, omelettes, salads. No reservations. Long queues form at weekends.
68 Greenwich Ave, between 7th Ave/11th St. Tel: (212) 243 1400.
Also at 183 Prince St, between Thompson/ Sullivan sts. Tel: (212) 260 3600.

CHINATOWN
Peking Duck House ★★
Peking duck in a plain setting; satisfying duck soups.
28 Mott St/Canal Square. Tel: (212) 227 1810.

The exotic Oyster Bar in Grand Central Station

Mueng Thai ★

Friendly service (not always encountered in Chinatown, where service can sometimes be too brisk and efficient) and remarkably low prices. Top-rate noodle dishes and spicy peanut sauce are among the specialities.

23 Pell Street, between Mott St/Bowery.
Tel: (212) 406 4259.

Oriental Pearl ★

Spacious but often busy, this is the place for *dim sum* and perfectly cooked vegetables.

103 Mott St, between Hester/Canal sts.
Tel: (212) 219 8388.

Wong Kee ★

No fancy decor, but bargain-basement prices for inspired Cantonese cooking.

113 Mott St, between Canal/Hester sts.
Tel: (212) 966 1160.

LITTLE ITALY
Angelo's ★★

Children are welcome in this typical Italian restaurant with a homely atmosphere and traditional southern Italian food.

146 Mulberry St, between Hester/Grand sts.
Tel: (212) 966 1277.

Il Cortile ★★

Very popular restaurant specialising in northern Italian cuisine, with an attractive conservatory-style dining room. Noteworthy veal and pasta dishes.

125 Mulberry St, between Canal/Hester sts.
Tel: (212) 226 6060.

CHELSEA & GRAMERCY
Lola ★★

Good American-Caribbean cuisine, but it is the music that counts. Calypso, reggae, jazz, and gospel music on Sunday.

30 W 22nd St, between 5th/6th aves. Tel: (212) 675 6700.

Mesa Grill ★★

Now an established house for southwestern grills.

102 5th Ave, between 15th/16th sts.
Tel: (212) 807 7400.

Old Town Bar ★

The food here is standard pub grub, but this traditional Victorian tavern is friendly, if noisy.

45 E 18th St, between Broadway/Park aves.
Tel: (212) 529 6732.

Periyali ★★

Better-than-average Greek restaurant, presenting herby grills – including octopus – and pleasantly informal.

35 W 20th St, between 5th/6th aves.
Tel: (212) 463 7890.

Union Square Café ★★★

Media people in the area flock to this ever-popular American restaurant.

21 E 16th St, between Union Square/5th Ave.
Tel: (212) 243 4020.

World Yacht Cruises ★★★

Dancing and continental cuisine aboard a luxury yacht cruising the waters around Manhattan.

Pier 81, W 41st St/ Hudson River.
Tel: (212) 630 8100.

Zen Palate ★★

A delight for vegetarians as tofu comes in many forms.

34 Union Square, E 16th St.
Tel: (212) 614 9345.

MEAT PACKING DISTRICT
Markt ★★

Fresh seafood at the raw bar, and sinful desserts.

401 W 14th St/9th Ave.
Tel: (212) 727 3314.

Fressen ★★★

Wholesome American food based on organic produce.

421 13th St between 9th Ave & Washington St.
Tel: (212) 645 7775.

Fast Food

Ask for a Coney Islander in a snack bar and you will probably get a puzzled stare. Invented about 100 years ago, it has long since changed its name to the hot dog, and out of hundreds of hot dog stands, probably the most famous is on Brooklyn's Coney Island, where it was invented.

New York City offers a good variety of fast food. The ubiquitous hamburger has travelled a long way since its origins in the small town of Hamburg in upstate New York, near Niagara Falls. Its predecessor was the pork pattie, but the two brothers who had a food concession at the 1885 Hamburg Fair ran out of pork, and improvised with minced beef, adding such unlikely things as brown sugar and coffee to get a satisfactory taste. Garnished with onions, catsup (ketchup), and mustard, it has been flavour of the decades ever since.

Jewish fast foods that most people enjoy are bagels and blintzes. Bagels are rings of hard bread, often toasted. Blintzes are crêpes filled with fruit or cheese and served with sour cream.

There is always a bite to eat on street corners. Pretzels and hot roast chestnuts

are popular. Many bars and diners offer free snacks with drinks during the weekday happy hour – usually a couple of hours. Or try one of the low-cost 24-hour eateries like Manhattan's Empire Diner at 210 Tenth Avenue and 22nd Street, where live piano music accompanies the simple American fare. Patsy's Pizza in East Harlem has a reputation for brick-oven pies with all fresh ingredients. Pastarias are all over town, and coffee shops are often good for home-cooked snacks.

Above: an American diner, as seen in a hundred movies; facing page & right: fast food fits the pace and style of this busy city

MIDTOWN

Afghan Kebab House ★
Take your own beer to cool down the after-effects of the spicy grilled kebabs.
155 W 46th St, between 6th/7th aves.
Tel: (212) 768 3875.

Aquavit ★★★
Scandinavian specialities – venison with juniper sauce, gravlax with mustard sauce – in former Rockefeller townhouse with a six-storey atrium with waterfall.
13 W 54th St, between 5th/6th aves.
Tel: (212) 307 7311.

Barbetta ★★★
Good Italian cuisine is served in elegantly formal surroundings in the heart of the Theater District. You can relax in the garden.
321 W 46th St, between 7th/9th aves.
Tel: (212) 246 9171.

Chez Napoléon ★★
Frogs' legs Provençale, bouillabaisse, and rabbit in wine are specialities.
365 W 50th St, between 8th/9th aves.
Tel: (212) 265 6980.

Fifty-seven Fifty-seven ★★★★
Heart-healthy American fare and killer martinis.
Four Seasons Hotel, 57 E 57th St.
Tel: (212) 758 5757.

Fino Ristorante ★★
In a modern setting, this northern Italian establishment serves hot antipasto, angel hair pasta with seafood sauce, and crostini de polenta as appetisers. Special dessert of pears with cinnamon and cherry syrup.
4 E 36th St, between 5th/Madison aves.
Tel: (212) 689 8040.

Four Seasons ★★★★
One of the world's great restaurants. Menus and decor change with the seasons, but the 24-foot long Picasso is always there. America's most complete wine cellar.
99 E 52nd St, between Park/Lexington aves.
Tel: (212) 754 9494.

Hakata ★
Round off a theatre trip with noodles and affordable sushi.
224 W 47th St, between Broadway/8th aves.
Tel: (212) 730 6863.

March ★★★
Serious American cuisine served as works of art in a townhouse setting. Sample warm chocolate cake with pistachio halva as a

grand finale to the optional fixed-price menu.
405 E 58th St, between 1st Ave/Sutton Place.
Tel: (212) 754 6272.

Oyster Bar & Restaurant ★★
One of New York's great experiences. Opened in 1913. Huge variety of delectable fresh fish, oyster stew, pan roasts, and desserts. Counter and table service.
Grand Central Station Lower Level, between Vanderbilt/Lexington aves.
Tel: (212) 490 6650.

Planet Hollywood ★
The bicycle from *Butch Cassidy and the Sundance Kid* and masses more film memorabilia are part of the decor at this high-vitality experience. Wide choice of good, quick food, plenty of it, and rich desserts.
140 W 57th St, between 6th/7th aves.
Tel: (212) 337 7827.

Remi ★★★
High-class Italian restaurant, where people go to see and be seen, and to enjoy the risotto and pasta.
145 W 53rd St, between 6th/7th aves.
Tel: (212) 581 4242.

Russian Samovar ★★
No-frills decor, but good food brings clients back again and again to this Theater District restaurant. Live Russian music with dinner.
256 W 52nd St, between Broadway/8th Ave.
Tel: (212) 757 0168.

Sardi's ★★
This Broadway legend continues to pull in the tourists and local inhabitants.
234 W 44th St, between Broadway/8th aves.
Tel: (212) 221 8444.

Victor's ★★
A Cuban classic in tropical setting. Stone crabs, paella, roast suckling pig, black bean soup in skylit rooms. Tapas bar. Soft piano music and a strolling violinist.
236 W 52nd St, between Broadway/8th Ave.
Tel: (212) 586 7714.

The View ★★★
No tourist should miss New York's only revolving restaurant, located high above Times Square. International cuisine. Pre-theatre menu is available. Worthwhile view.
Marriott Marquis Hotel, 1535 Broadway, between 45th/46th sts.
Tel: (212) 704 8900.

Woo Chon ★
A range of authentic hearty dishes at great value at this convivial Korean restaurant with a waterfall feature. Delicious seafood pancakes are among the foods on the menu.
8–10 W 36th St, between 5th/6th aves.
Tel: (212) 695 0676.

Wylie's Ribs ★
A place 'to get stuck in'. Nobody leaves hungry. Serves mouth-watering barbecue foods. Not the place for vegetarians.
891 1st Ave/50th St.
Tel: (212) 751 0700.

Victor's on 52nd Street

EAST SIDE

Afghan Kebab House ★

High-value, low-cost kebabs and other savoury ethnic food. Bring your own alcoholic beverage.
1345 2nd Ave, between 70th/71st sts.
Tel: (212) 517 2776.

Café Greco ★★

Mediterranean dishes from France, Italy, North Africa, and Greece. Also high-value fixed-price option – all in an attractive, split-level atrium setting.
1390 2nd Ave, between 71st/72nd sts.
Tel: (212) 737 4300.

Le Perigord ★★★

Aficionados say this is one of the best classic French restaurants in town. It has offered a fine dining experience for many years. Do make a reservation.
405 E 52nd St/1st Ave.
Tel: (212) 755 6244.

Mark's ★★★

Another established favourite at the top end of the scale, with two tiers of tables in a very relaxed atmosphere. Innovative menu – red snapper on eggplant caviar, for example, or roast pheasant with celery root mousseline and calvados sauce.
Mark Hotel, 25 E 77th St/Madison Ave.
Tel: (212) 879 1864.

Mocca Hungarian ★

Homely, filling food generously served in this bit of old Yorkville.
1588 2nd Ave, between 82nd/83rd sts.
Tel: (212) 734 6470.

The Pie ★

Not enough space to spread yourself about, but Russian specialities like kasha, stuffed cabbage, and chicken kiev leave you replete and content.
340 E 86th St, between 1st/2nd aves.
Tel: (212) 517 8717.

Pig Heaven ★★

Pork (as you might have guessed) is the speciality in this popular Chinese East Sider.
1540 2nd Ave, between 80th/81st sts.
Tel: (212) 744 4333.

Pinocchio ★★

The locals like this restaurant, where candles gleam, music from the opera provides a pleasant background, and good Italian food satisfies.
170 E 81st St, between Lexington/3rd aves.
Tel: (212) 650 1513.

Post House ★★★

An American steakhouse par excellence. Superior wine list, beef served 10 different ways, and superb seafood. Try chilled baby lobster as an appetiser.

SUNDAY BRUNCH

This is an institution in New York. Some restaurants provide full waiter service. Others offer buffet-style food beautifully displayed.

Brunchtime varies slightly, but is usually somewhere between 11am and 4pm.

'Eat where the locals go' is always good advice. The Mark Hotel has a loyal following among its neighbours in E 77th Street and Madison Avenue area. With visitors, too, it is busy every Sunday at brunchtime.

Choose from the menu – crabmeat salad, duckling hash, brioche French toast, and bow tie pasta with mushrooms and asparagus are among the options – or go for prix fixe, with a choice of two or three courses.

*28 E 63rd St, between
Madison/Park aves.
Tel: (212) 935 2888.*
Sarah Beth's Kitchen ★★
Informal dining in
pleasant, home-like, no-
smoking atmosphere.
Interesting menus.
*1295 Madison Ave,
between 92nd/93rd sts.
Tel: (212) 410 7335.
Also at Whitney Museum,*

*945 Madison Ave/
75th St.
Tel: (212) 570 3670.*
Urban Grill ★
A great place for the
simple things, like pastas
and burgers; also take-
out food.
*1613 2nd Ave, between
83rd/84th sts.
Tel: (212) 744 2122.
Also at 330 W 58th St,*

*between 8th/9th aves.
Tel: (212) 586 3300.*
Vico ★★
Vivid and noisy, and not
cheap, this Italian
restaurant nevertheless
attracts the crowds
because the food is
consistently inspired.
*1302 Madison Ave/
92nd St.
Tel: (212) 876 2222.*

Café with a patriotic air

Cheers!

Twice every day and once on Sunday, the most popular of New York's many, many bars shift into top gear. On weekdays they fill up at lunchtime with people from shops and offices who gulp a beer or glass of wine and grab a snack; when work is over, the same people will be back for a more leisurely 'happy hour' (which often lasts for more than an hour; 5–7pm is a typical duration), ending the day in entertaining gossip and character assassination. Like delis and subway stations, bars are an essential facet of New York life. Miss them, and you are missing New York.

At weekends, bars offering brunch will be busy from noon until around 4pm. The bar in its many forms is a New York institution, ranging from the quiet and dignified watering holes for the rich and powerful at the Wall Street end of town, to the cheap and cheerful (or maybe not so cheerful) dives dotted about all over the place.

For sports fans who like to do their

spectating the easy way, there are special bars with huge TV sets tuned to the big match. Singles bars are no longer dominated by hopeful lone souls arranged along bar stools. These days, the accent is on having fun while seeking new friends.

In the Christopher Street area of Greenwich Village many of the bars are the haunt of gays and lesbians. Café life in New York comes plain or with a piano, romantic or rowdy, gentle or with rock, out of doors or by the fire, and in a whole captivating range of ethnic styles.

Whatever your mood, there is a café to meet it. People-watching – whether it is done in an Irish bar with an unkempt group belting out songs from the Ould Country, or in a café with a sedate jazz trio – costs nothing. The passing scene is bound to fascinate first-timers in the city, and eavesdroppers will have the time of their life.

Happy Hour – like baseball and hot dogs, the bar is an American classic

WEST SIDE

American Festival Café ★★

Classical American cooking served with a view of the ice rink or summer garden, depending on season.
Rockefeller Center,
20 W 50th St.
Tel: (212) 246 6699.

Bangkok Cuisine ★

This was New York's first Thai restaurant and continues to produce the right flavour.
885 8th Ave, between
52nd & 53rd sts.
Tel: (212) 581 6370.

Café des Artistes ★★★

Opened in 1917 in an historic building with nymphs cavorting around the walls, this restaurant across the street from ABC and near the Lincoln Center attracts celebrities. Superior food and service.
1 W 67th St, off Central
Park West.
Tel: (212) 877 3500.

Cleopatra's Needle ★

Not great on character but a reliable choice for good Middle Eastern food.
2485 Broadway/92nd St.
Tel: (212) 769 6969.

Cotton Club ★★

The Harlem legend is back in business, serving soul food from the South and a hot gospel ambience for Sunday brunch.

656 W 125th St, between
Broadway/Riverside Drive.
Tel: (212) 663 7980.

Darbar ★★

Well above average Indian restaurant specialising in tandoori dishes, *saag gosht,* crab Malabar, and lamb kebab Punjabi.
44 W 56th St at
5th & 6th aves.
Tel: (212) 432 7227.

Dish of Salt ★★

Multi-level Cantonese. Specialities include Peking duck, lobster, dumplings, steak Kew.
133 W 47th St between
6th & 7th aves.
Tel: (212) 921 4242.

Ellen's Stardust ★

Back to the 1950s with shake, rattle, and roll and vintage '50s music. Pink Lady cocktails and grilled swordfish steaks.
1650 Broadway/51st St.
Tel: (212) 956 5151.

Frankie and Johnnie's ★★

Landmark restaurant famous for steaks, chops, and seafood since 1926.
269 W 45th St.
Tel: (212) 977 9494.

Hurley's Saloon ★★

Established in 1892, this seafood and steak house serves memorable veal O'Neill, stuffed shrimps, and steak au poivre.
1240 6th Ave at 49th St.
Tel: (212) 765 8981.

THE GREAT AMERICAN BREAKFAST

Oh, the great American breakfast! In New York you can pop into a diner for a sustaining pile of pancakes with maple syrup for less than $5. Or you can go to a classy restaurant for the works.

How is this, for instance? Granola with berries or smoked salmon with cream cheese and bagels. Eggs Benedict or corned beef hash with egg, or smoked salmon omelette, or prime breakfast sirloin with eggs. You will almost certainly get a basket of breads, Danish pastries, fruit preserves, and honey included in the cost.

Then there is coffee. Be prepared for the inquiry: 'Caff? Decaff? With milk? OK, skim? Semi-skim? Full cream?'

HoHo ★

Cantonese and Mandarin dishes in modern setting. Try stuffed crab claw, sate beef, or Kung Pao lobster Ting.

131 W 50th St at 6th &
7th aves.
Tel: (212) 246 3256.

Jean Lafitte ★★

Parisian-style bistro serving French and continental cuisine. Evening entertainment, live jazz.

68 W 58th St, between
5th & 6th aves.
Tel: (212) 751 2323.

Joe Allen ★

Theatrical habitat which brings out the stars and the stargazers.

326 W 46th St between
8th & 9th aves.
Tel: (212) 581 6464.

Kaplan's Delicatessen ★

Jewish-style deli restaurant. Specialities: Romanian steak, pastrami, chicken in pot, stuffed cabbage, potato pancakes.

W 47th St at 5th & 6th
aves. Tel: (212) 391 2333.

La Fondue ★

Cheese fondues, Swiss chocolate fondues, quiches, and irresistible desserts. Casual.

43 W 55th St between
5th & 6th aves.
Tel: (212) 581 0820.

Le Relais ★★

Parisian-style bistro, attracting the young set. In summer the half-dozen sidewalk tables are much in demand by people-watchers.

712 Madison Ave between
63rd & 64th sts.
Tel: (212) 751 5108.

Le Rivage ★★

Generous portions of traditional bistro fare which many consider to be the best French buy in the Theater District. The fixed-price dinner is a bargain.

340 W 46th St, between
8th/9th aves.
Tel: (212) 765 7374.

Nirvana ★★

Flavourful Indo-Bengali fare in a 15th-floor penthouse with superb views.

30 Central Park S.
Tel: (212) 486 5700.

Pasha ★★★

Traditional Turkish lamb, quail, and aubergine-based cuisine.

170 W 71st St.
Tel: (212) 579 8751.

Petrossian ★★★★

The Petrossian family is a leading importer of caviar to the USA, and the ornate restaurant entices gourmets with pre- and post-theatre offerings of Beluga, Ostera, and Sevruga caviar – now a rarity.

182 W 58th St/7th Ave.
Tel: (212) 245 2214.

Sfuzzi ★★

Italian American food – pizzas, pastas, salads, and grilled dishes. High-tech lighting dramatises the brick walls. Located near Lincoln Center and ABC – this is surely the place to spot the stars.

58 W 65th St, between
Central Park/Columbus
Ave. Tel: (212) 873 3700.

Sushi Zen ★★

Elegantly served sushi in a tranquil setting.

57 W 46th St between
5th/6th aves.
Tel: (212) 302 0707.

The River Café – good food in superb surroundings

HARLEM
La Famille ★★
As well as Harlem soul food, you have the option of continental dishes in this upstairs restaurant. Downstairs the jazz music beats out.
2017 5th Ave between 124th/125th sts.
Tel: (212) 722 9806.

Patsy's Pizza ★
All-fresh ingredients go into the pizzas baked in a brick oven, and send Patsy's patrons into raptures.
2287 1st Ave between 117th/118th sts.
Tel: (212) 534 9783.

Sylvia's Soul Food Restaurant ★
Southern staples like spicy barbecued ribs, fried chicken, pecan pie, and greens to set you alight.
328 Malcolm X Blvd between 126th/127th sts.
Tel: (212) 996 0660.

BRONX
Dominik's ★
Communal tables, no menu, and plenty of fun and southern Italian food for everyone.
2335 Arthur Ave between 186th/187th sts.
Tel: (718) 733 2807.

QUEENS
Benjamin's ★★
Specialities from American regions. Lively entertainment.
LaGuardia Marriott, 102–05 Ditmars Blvd, East Elmhurst.
Tel: (718) 565 8900.

Piccola Venezia ★★
Sustaining authentic Italian food in a busy, bustling setting.
42–01 28th Ave/42nd St.
Tel: (718) 721 8470.

Quartier ★
Pleasant dining at Forest Hills.
107–02 Queens Blvd/ 70th Ave.
Tel: (718) 520 8037.

Water's Edge ★★
Contemporary American cuisine. Formal dining aboard a barge with the Manhattan skyline viewed across the water.
44th Drive East River, Long Island City.
Tel: (718) 936 7110.

BROOKLYN
Gage & Tollner ★★
Virginia specialities – she-crab soup, gumbo, pan-fried quail. Soft gas lamps illuminate the long-established 'interior landmark' restaurant.
372 Fulton St between Adams and Jay sts.
Tel: (718) 875 5181.

Henry's End ★★
American cooking with a French accent on fish and game.
44 Henry St/Cranberry St.
Tel: (718) 834 1776.

101 ★
The young locals thrive on pizza and pasta at this cheerful eatery.
10018 4th Ave/101st St.
Tel: (718) 833 1313.

Paradise ★★
A favourite for many years, with its old-fashioned Russian ambience.
8017 5th Ave, between 80th/81st sts.
Tel: (718) 921 0266.

Peter Luger Steakhouse ★★★
The big T-bone steaks at this no-frills 1887 restaurant. The dull decor and plain scrubbed oak tables do not deter the crowds.
178 Broadway/Driggs Ave.
Tel: (718) 387 7400.

Queen ★★
A meeting place for discriminating judges and lawyers.
84 Court St, between Livingstone & Schermerhorn sts.
Tel: (718) 596 5955.

River Café ★★★★
Highly prestigious restaurant with one of New York's most creative chefs. Sample his vegetable-stuffed scallops with curry oil and fennel seed, followed by salmon seared with ginger and cracked pepper, Burgundy butter, and lotus chips.
1 Water St, under Brooklyn Bridge, Brooklyn Heights.
Tel: (718) 522 5200.

Tripoli ★
The food is affordable and dependable and the belly dancers add relish.
156 Atlantic Ave/Clinton St. Tel: (718) 596 5800.

STATEN ISLAND
Lum Chin ★
Good Chinese food served in a tastefully decorated interior. There is a wide variety to choose from.
4326 Amboy Rd, between Richard/Armstrong aves.
Tel: (718) 984 8044.

Terrace Grill ★★
On the edge of New York Harbor, this restaurant with a view of Manhattan offers casual eating, from light lunch to full dinner. Entertainment.
44 Richmond Terrace.
Tel: (718) 720 8948.

The best of Chinese cuisine

Hotels and Accommodation

Whatever bargains New York may offer, accommodation is unlikely to be among them. The city has plenty of comfortable places where visitors can lay their heads at night – at least 59,000 hotel rooms, it has been estimated – but there are not so many at the lower end of the price scale. Be prepared to shop around.

The Plaza, 5th Avenue at Central Park South

Real estate and labour are weighty items in any New York hotel's overheads, and are reflected in its tariff. However, standards of accommodation and service are exceptionally high, though rooms might not be so spacious as elsewhere in the USA, and car parking, of course, is seriously restricted and expensive.

Stylish hotels are seldom for the budget-conscious

Deluxe hotels have superbly furnished rooms, equipped with such amenities as satellite television (with a set in the bathroom, too), sophisticated telephone systems, fax machine points, and internet access – to say nothing of king-size beds (often two).

The price you pay in a New York hotel is for a double room per night, excluding taxes; breakfast is rarely included. Many rooms have self-catering facilities – refrigerator, cooker, micro-wave oven, and dishwasher – and some will have a washing machine and drier.

At long last, New York City has lifted the ban on minibars in hotel rooms. They were previously illegal because they provided access to alcohol to those who could check into a hotel at 18, but were below the minimum drinking age of 21.

Many hotels have fitness centres, or will make arrangements nearby, but few have their own swimming pools – the precious space factor again.

Guests can usually negotiate a special weekly rate, and hotels catering mainly for business clients often offer up to 50 per cent discount for a weekend stopover. This can be a great saving for a family, and it might well be worth checking into a junior suite with more room and even better amenities.

Whatever room rate is agreed, remember that at the end of your stay local sales tax (8.25 per cent at the time of writing) will be added to the account. Hefty surcharges for telephone calls made from your room will also boost the final tally, and from arrival to departure you will be expected to tip, tip, tip.

Where to Stay

Many of the city's best hotels are in the midtown area, lying between Third Avenue/40th St and Seventh Avenue/60th St. The most prestigious properties are on the Upper East Side north of 59th St, where the best known museums, art galleries, and boutiques are to be found.

Theatre buffs will find a convenient cluster of well-known hotels straddling Broadway between 42nd and 57th Sts,

all handy for the Lincoln Center and Carnegie Hall, as well as the major playhouses.

Moderately priced yet comfortable accommodation can be found in Murray Hill, a quiet area east of Fifth Avenue between 34th and 42nd Sts. If you don't mind being out of town, there are motels near the airports. The *Time Out New York* website is an excellent guide to help you find places to stay to suit your needs (*www.timeoutny.com*).

Dress and Behaviour

Even those visitors who are on holiday will be expected by the management of better hotels to fall in with a basic decorum and dress code. Men are expected to wear jackets – and ties, too, frequently – in dining rooms and bars after 5pm or 6pm. Those slopping around in shorts or beachwear may find themselves being served frostily, or even being ignored altogether. Extreme offenders may be asked to leave.

The beautiful Carlyle Hotel at Madison Avenue

Cheaper Options

Flophouses apart, it is not easy to find cheap accommodation in New York. The choice is largely limited to the YMCA/YWCA (the 'Y'), youth hostels, and one or two student centres. Another option now beginning to open up is Bed and Breakfast in private homes, though it would be fairer to describe these generally as excellent value for money rather than cheap.

Youth Hostels

The 'Y' has three centres in Manhattan, each safe and well placed with simple, clean accommodation and good facilities, such as restaurants and laundromats. Tourist package deals are available. The **McBurney Y** (Chelsea at 206 W 24th St, *tel: (212) 741 9226*) has 250 rooms, of which 215 are singles. The

The Chelsea Hotel, 222 West 23rd Street

A chauffeur waits outside the Plaza

larger **Vanderbilt Y** (224 E 47th St, *tel: (212) 756 9600*) is close to Grand Central Station and has a pool and gym.

The **West Side Y** (W 63rd St, between Broadway and Central Park West, *tel: (212) 787 4400*) also has a full range of facilities, and is handy for the Upper West Side and Lincoln Center.

The best of the hostels is the **International Youth Hostel** opened by American Youth Hostels in a renovated 19th-century Gothic-style building (891 Amsterdam Ave at 103rd St, *tel: (212) 932 2300*). Facilities include a restaurant, laundromat, travel shop, and meeting rooms. The hostel is well placed for Columbus University and Harlem.

International House of New York is a large hostel with good facilities and clean dormitory and room accommodation (500 Riverside Drive, *tel: (212) 316 8400*). Prospective guests will need to prove they are genuine students, though this may be waived at slack times.

Bed and Breakfast

Belatedly, the city is following the B&B trend already well established in many other parts of the USA, especially upstate New York. Although they are considerably cheaper than Manhattan hotels, B&B prices are far from rock-bottom. But standards are generally very high, and it is not unusual for rooms to be equipped with telephone, TV and radio, and en suite bathroom. Jacuzzis and pools are not unknown.

The chief attraction of B&B is that visitors get the chance to take a close-up look at backyard New York. Hosts, often retired or professional people whose children have flown the nest, can be immensely hospitable and helpful, providing a seemingly endless fund of local knowledge.

Breakfast is usually a leisurely, conversational time when lots of information is swapped around the table. The mood is informal, and guests are free to come and go as they please. B&B accommodation is not usually advertised on porches or in windows as you may find elsewhere. It is usual in New York to make reservations well in advance through an agency. Agencies based in the city are:

Bed and Breakfast Network of New York (Suite 602, 134 W 32nd St, *tel: (212) 645 8134).*

New World Bed and Breakfast (Suite 711, 150 5th Ave, *tel: (212) 675 5600).*

New Yorkers At Home (301 E 60th St, *tel: (212) 838 7015).*

Urban Ventures (306 W 38th St, *tel: (212) 594 5650).*

Whichever form of accommodation you choose, it is important to make early reservations.

The Wyndham Hotel, 100–15 Ditmars Boulevard, East Elmhurst

Practical Guide

Arriving

Documentation

Passports are required by all visitors to the USA; visas are required by all except Canadians, New Zealanders, and UK citizens visiting for business or tourism for a stay of not more than 90 days, and providing that an onward or return ticket is held, and that they are arriving in the USA on a participating carrier. UK citizens and New Zealanders must also have completed a visa waiver form. Whilst in the USA, visitors can take a side trip overland or by sea to Canada or Mexico and re-enter the USA without a visa within the 90-day period. This rule also applies to nationals of most other European and Scandinavian countries, and Japan. Travellers who do need a visa should send an application form (obtainable from travel agents or the American Embassy) to the visa department of the American Embassy in their own country.

By Air

New York is served by three airports: John F Kennedy International and LaGuardia, both in Queens, and Newark International in New Jersey. LaGuardia mainly handles domestic services. A recorded information service covering all three airports is operated by the Port Authority of New York and New Jersey (*tel: (800) 247 7433*).

Airport Transfers

JFK is 15 miles from mid-Manhattan. **Carey Buses** (*tel: (718) 632 0500*) runs a half-hourly express service from the airport to Grand Central Terminal between 6am and midnight, and in the opposite direction between 5am and 1am. The journey takes around an hour. A Carey Express also runs hourly (7am–7pm) between JFK and Williamsburg, Brooklyn.

The Port Authority shuttle bus is free and runs every 20 minutes (5am to midnight) to the Howard Beach Station (*tel: (718) 330 1234*) for the price of a subway token ($1.50). Arriving passengers can take the A train to Brooklyn and Manhattan.

Public buses operated by **Green Bus Lines** (*tel: (718) 995 4700*) run from JFK terminals to subway stations at Lefferts Boulevard (trains to Brooklyn, Lower and West Side Manhattan) and Kew Gardens/Union Turnpike (Queens and mid-Manhattan). The service is Q-10, and buses run every 15 minutes, 24 hours a day.

The M60 bus runs every 20 minutes from all terminals, through Queens, over the Triborough Bridge and into Manhattan and onto 125th Street. The final destination is Broadway and 106th Street. The current price for a bus and subway ticket is $1.50.

A taxi trip to midtown Manhattan takes about an hour, and costs a flat rate of $35 plus toll tax plus tip. Fares between destinations in New York City and LaGuardia or Kennedy airports are metered. In yellow cabs between the city and Newark Airport, the fare is the amount shown on the meter plus $10 at the time of writing. Bridge and tunnel tolls are extra charges.

New York Helicopter offers frequent flights from the two international airports to the E 34th Street Heliport at First Avenue.

La Guardia has a water taxi service. The Delta Water Shuttle operates half-hourly between the Marine Air Terminal and the East River at 34th Street, and to Pier 11 in Manhattan's financial district. Newark, 16 miles from Manhattan, has two bus services and a bus rail link.

New Jersey Transit (*tel: (800) 772 2222*) runs a 24-hour express bus service every 15 or 30 minutes to the Port Authority Terminal in Manhattan.

Olympia Trails Airport Express (*tel: (212) 964 6233*) has a service every 20 minutes between 5am and 1am, with stops at the Port Authority, and Grand Central and Pennsylvania stations.

PATH Rapid Transit (*1 800 234 PATH*) operates a shuttle bus train link between the airport, Newark's Penn station, and stations in Manhattan.

By Sea
QEII and cruise ship passengers arrive in mid-Manhattan at the Passenger Ship Terminal which extends from 48th to 52nd streets. The air-conditioned terminal has streamlined baggage-handling and customs facilities, and bus connections to Midtown.

By Rail
Long-haul services (Amtrak), New Jersey Transit, and Long Island Railroad trains use Penn Station as a terminal. Local and commuter services use both Penn and Grand Central Station.

By Bus
The Port Authority Bus Terminal at Eighth Avenue, between 40th/42nd streets, handles long-distance and commuter services (*tel: (212) 564 8484*).

Children
New York's subways and buses are free for children under the age of six. Babysitting services can usually be arranged through your hotel, or through such agencies as Convention Kids Inc, 340 E 93rd Street, Suite 12E (*tel: (212) 289 0035*).

Climate
The city's climate is described as temperate, a fact many will contemplate ruefully at each end of the weather spectrum: in January, when the mean temperature is 32°F (0°C), and July when the streets are stickily humid in an average temperature of 77°F (25°C).

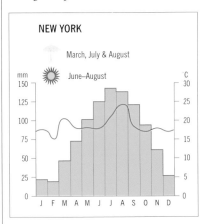

NEW YORK

March, July & August

June–August

Weather Conversion Chart
25.4mm = 1 inch
°F = 1.8 x °C + 32

Crime

There is plenty of petty crime in New York and, as in any big city, strangers are easy prey. The best way to avoid being mugged is to avoid lonely, dark places. Do not travel on the subway at night on your own. Some deprived areas, like the South Bronx, should be avoided altogether; others, like Harlem, are best visited on a guided tour. Never carry more money than you are likely to need when you go out. If you do get mugged and/or robbed, call a cab and ask to be taken to the nearest police station. The police will file a report which will help with any insurance claim you may make.

The ubiquitous yellow cab

Customs Regulations

The duty-free allowances for non-US residents over the age of 21 are 200 cigarettes, or 100 cigars, or 3lb of tobacco or any proportionate combination; one US quart of spirits or wine, and up to $100 worth of duty-free gifts (including up to 100 cigars), provided the traveller is staying in the USA for at least 72 hours. Articles should not be gift-wrapped. Prohibited goods include meat and meat products, dairy products, fruit, plants, seeds, drugs, lottery tickets, and obscene publications.

Driving

If driving in the city is unavoidable, make sure you understand the restrictions, because penalties for infringements are stringent. In many streets, parking alternates daily from one side to the other, and it is illegal to park within 10 feet either side of a fire hydrant. A car illegally parked will be towed away by one of the city's super-efficient contract crews, and the driver will be fined heavily. Never leave anything in an unguarded vehicle.

Breakdowns

Services of the American Automobile Association (AAA) are free to members of affiliated motoring organisations. New York City's branch is at 28 E 78th Street (*tel: (212) 586 1166*); open: Mon–Fri 9.30am–5.30pm. The AAA nationwide emergency number is *1 800 336 HELP*.

Car Rental

All the major rental companies have centres in New York, especially at the airports. Hirers will need to have a full valid UK or EU driving licence, and a major credit card or hefty cash deposit. They must also be at least 25 years old (only 21 if you rent in New Jersey or Connecticut). Car rental is not cheap, but some discounts exist for weekend rentals. Make car reservations before entering the USA for the best deal.

Ensure that you are covered for liability to third parties in a driving accident, either by purchasing insurance from the rental company, or by taking out top-up insurance from your travel agent. Ordinary travel insurance does not provide this cover.

Fuel

The American pint is 20 per cent smaller than the imperial measure, which means five gallons of petrol ('gas') is about four UK gallons or 18 litres. Petrol is about half the UK price, and gas stations, many of which stay open 24 hours, usually require payment before allowing you to fill up.

The Law

Drive on the right, do not exceed the speed limits, and do not drink and drive. Alcohol belonging to the driver or passengers must be kept in the boot. The upper speed limit on interstate highways in New York State is 65mph, but lower limits may apply on other types of road. The city limit is 20–25mph. Seat belts are compulsory. Passing a stopped school bus (usually yellow with flashing red lights) is illegal, and stiff fines can be imposed.

Electricity

110–115 volts AC, 60 cycles AC. Sockets ('outlets') take plugs with two flat-pin connections.

Embassies and Consulates

Australian Consulate

636 5th Ave. *Tel: (212) 245 4000.*

Ireland Consulate

515 Madison Ave. *Tel: (212) 319 2555.*

UK Consulate

845 3rd Ave. *Tel: (212) 752 8400.*

Police presence on the streets is reassuring

Someone's 15 minutes of fame

Emergency Telephone Numbers

Ambulance, Fire Brigade, or Police: *911.*
Medical emergencies: *(212) 238 2100.*
Dental emergencies: *(212) 679 3966.*
MasterCard card loss or theft: *1 800 307 7309 (toll free).*
Thomas Cook Traveller's Cheques loss or theft (report within 24 hours): *1 800 223 7373 (toll free).*

Entertainment Information

Village Voice, published Wednesdays and available free of charge, lists all New York entertainments, as does the Weekend section of Friday's *New York Times*. Other sources: *New Yorker* and *New York Magazine.*

Discount Tickets

Entertainment in New York is not cheap, but there are ways of reducing the cost. Half-price tickets for Broadway and Off-Broadway shows are sold on the day of performance at TKTS booths in Times Square and near Borough Hall in Brooklyn.

The main booth, in Times Square, starts selling tickets for that day's matinees at 10am, but queue early to avoid disappointment. Tickets for evening performances are available from 3–8pm, Monday to Saturday. The booths at Montague and Court Streets in Brooklyn sell some matinee tickets the day before the performance. Opening time for the Brooklyn booth is Monday to Friday 11.30am–5.30pm, Saturday 11am–3pm.

Health

Vaccinations are not required for entry into the United States, but visitors are strongly advised to take out medical insurance cover. Doctors are listed in the *Yellow Pages* under 'Clinics' or 'Physicians and Surgeons'. Emergency departments open 24 hours a day:

Bellevue Hospital
1st Ave/E 29th St. *Tel: (212) 561 4141.*
St Vincent's Hospital
7th Ave/11th St. *Tel: (212) 790 7000 or 7997.*
New York Hospital E 70th St/York Ave. *Tel: (212) 472 5050.*
Mount Sinai Hospital, Madison Ave/100th St. *Tel: (212) 241 7171.*
You can also call: **NY Hotel Urgent Medical Services** (*tel: (212) 737 1212*). AIDS is a big problem in New York City, as it is worldwide, and the need to practise safe sex cannot be over-emphasised.

Insurance

Travel

You should take out personal travel insurance before leaving, from your travel agent, tour operator, or insurance company. It should give adequate cover for medical expenses, loss and theft, personal liability (but liability arising from motor accidents is not usually included – see below), and cancellation expenses. Always read the conditions, which include any exclusions and details of cover, and check that the amount of cover is adequate. Remember that medical treatment can be very expensive in the USA.

Driving

If you hire a car, collision insurance, often called collision damage waiver or CDW, is normally offered by the hirer, and is usually compulsory. Check with your own motor insurers before you leave, as you may be covered by your normal policy. If not, CDW is payable locally, and may be as much as 50 per cent of the hiring fee. Neither CDW nor your personal travel insurance will protect you from liability arising out of an accident in a hire car, for example, if you damage another vehicle, or injure someone. If you are likely to hire a car, you should obtain such extra cover, preferably from your travel agent or other insurer before departure.

Maps and Guides

The **New York City Convention and Visitors' Bureau**, 2 Columbus Circle, NY10019, (*tel: (212) 397 8200 or 8222*) has information on almost everything that goes on in the city, as well as transport and accommodation details. The bureau is open Monday to Friday 9am–6pm, weekends and public holidays 10am–6pm. More information is available from the **I Love New York** office at 1515 Broadway, NY10036, (*tel: (212) 827 6250*). Street maps are sold in bookshops, and easy to use laminated maps can be purchased for under $6.

Conversion Table

FROM	TO	MULTIPLY BY
Inches	Centimetres	2.54
Feet	Metres	0.3048
Yards	Metres	0.9144
Miles	Kilometres	1.6090
Acres	Hectares	0.4047
Gallons	Litres	4.5460
Ounces	Grams	28.35
Pounds	Grams	453.6
Pounds	Kilograms	0.4536
Tons	Tonnes	1.0160

To convert back, for example from centimetres to inches, divide by the number in the third column.

Men's Suits

UK	36	38	40	42	44	46	48
Rest of Europe	46	48	50	52	54	56	58
USA	36	38	40	42	44	46	48

Dress Sizes

UK	8	10	12	14	16	18
France	36	38	40	42	44	46
Italy	38	40	42	44	46	48
Rest of Europe	34	36	38	40	42	44
USA	6	8	10	12	14	16

Men's Shirts

UK	14	14.5	15	15.5	16	16.5	17
Rest of Europe	36	37	38	39/40	41	42	43
USA	14	14.5	15	15.5	16	16.5	17

Men's Shoes

UK	7	7.5	8.5	9.5	10.5	11
Rest of Europe	41	42	43	44	45	46
USA	8	8.5	9.5	10.5	11.5	12

Women's Shoes

UK	4.5	5	5.5	6	6.5	7
Rest of Europe	38	38	39	39	40	41
USA	6	6.5	7	7.5	8	8.5

Measurements and Sizes
The USA has Imperial measurements.

Media
The *New York Times* is a multi-section broadsheet with daily and Sunday editions. The city has two tabloids, the *New York Post*, which likes to sensationalise things, and the *Daily News*. The only national daily newspaper is the *USA Today*, but in New York the *New York Times* makes more impact. The *Wall Street Journal*, New York based, carries national and international news as well as financial reports. For the visitor, the *New York* magazine or the popular weekly magazines *The New Yorker* and *Time Out New York* are good buys.

Quality documentaries, plays, and educational programmes are on Public Broadcasting Services' Channels 5, 13, 25, and 31.

The most popular Cable TV programmes are the 24-hour Cable News Network, the films on HBO (Home Box Office), and music on MTV (Music Television).

Money Matters
A dollar is made up of 100 cents, with coins of 1 cent (a penny), 5 cents (nickel), 10 cents (dime), and 25 cents (quarter). The quarter is the most useful coin for slot machines, telephones, and parking meters.

Dollar bills come in denominations of 1, 2, 5, 10, 20, 50, and 100, and they are all exactly the same in size and colour, except that each carries a portrait of a different US president. Any amount of dollars may be imported or exported, but amounts larger than $10,000 – in cash or gold – must be reported to US Customs.

JFK International Airport bureaux de change are located at:
West Wing, International Arrivals Building (*tel: (718) 656 8444*). Open daily 2–10pm.
Delta Terminal, Cart B2. Open daily noon–8pm.
Delta Terminal, Cart B6. Open daily 1.30–9.30pm.
Delta Terminal, Cart B9. Open daily 1–8pm.

Thomas Cook traveller's cheques are readily recognised in New York, and accepted for encashment or transactions in most hotels and many shops. But you should make sure that they are US currency cheques.

The branches of Thomas Cook listed on page 190 will change currency and Thomas Cook traveller's cheques free of commission.

Banking hours are usually Monday to Friday 9am–3pm (sometimes until 4pm). Some banks stay open later on Fridays, or open on Saturday mornings.

The USA runs on plastic money, and 'major credit cards' are a requirement when checking into a hotel, or renting a car. Cards can also be used in automated teller machines (ATMs).

National Holidays
Busy holiday times:
1 January New Year's Day
February, third Monday President's Day
May, last Monday Memorial Day
4 July Independence Day
September, first Monday Labor Day
October, second Monday Columbus Day
11 November Veterans' Day

November, fourth Thursday
Thanksgiving
25 December Christmas Day

Organised Tours

The best way to get the most out of New York is to tour on foot, and a number of companies and special interest organisations exist which arrange walking tours for groups, usually led by an expert in a particular area or subject.

Art Tours of New York (*tel: (212) 677 6005*) conducts informative tours of the galleries of SoHo, 57th Street, and Madison Avenue, and arranges visits to studios and galleries.

The Bronx County Historical Society (*tel: (718) 881 8900*) and Brooklyn Historical Society (*tel: (718) 864 0890*) both lead strolling tours of the highlights of their respective areas. In Central Park the Urban Rangers (*tel: (212) 360 2774*) organise a year-round programme of free educational walks.

Two companies specialise in tours of Harlem. Harlem Spirituals Inc (*tel: (212) 757 0425*) takes visitors on Sunday morning visits to a Baptist church, and night-time dinner and music events.

Sidewalks of New York (*tel: (212) 662 5300*) has a number of walks covering famous murder locations, and the homes of celebrities. Big Onion provides an array of interesting, informative, and inexpensive (under $12) walking tours throughout the city. Tour guides are usually doctoral students at Columbia University (*tel: (212) 439 1090; www.bigonion.com*).

Bus Tours

Gray Line (*tel: (212) 397 2620*) has been conducting tours of New York for more than half a century, and its current selection of about 25 tours covers everything from a trip to Radio City Music Hall to journeys up the Hudson Valley, and to the casinos of Atlantic City in New Jersey.

The Manhattan Neighbourhood Trolley is a restored vintage bus in which tourists visit the major sights, including the Financial District, Chinatown, and Little Italy.

Boat Tours

Circle Line (*tel: (212) 563 3200*) offers a three-hour circumnavigation of Manhattan Island. Trips operate from the Hudson River end of 42nd Street several times a day. Seaport Line (*tel: (212) 233 4800*) has a programme of 90-minute cruises off Lower Manhattan and the nearby islands. Cheapest of all, of course, is the Staten Island Ferry.

Helicopter Tours

Island Helicopter (*tel: (212) 683 4575*) and Liberty Helicopter Tours (*tel: (212) 629 5370*) offer breathtaking day- and night-time flights.

No, not the wrong picture – just a bus tour of New York

directory

Pharmacies

Medication for minor ailments and injuries can be obtained at drugstores and pharmacies, found on almost every block. They also sell a wide range of cosmetics, toiletries, sanitary items, and contraceptives. Usual opening hours are 9am–6pm, Monday to Saturday, but a 24-hour service is provided by Kaufman, 557 Lexington Avenue at 50th Street (*tel: (212) 755 2266*).

Places of Worship

New York has more than 2,500 places of worship, and every religious denomination is represented. Look in the *Yellow Pages*, or ask the concierge at your hotel.

Police

Police headquarters are in the Civic Center. In an emergency, dial 911 or use one of the clearly marked street police telephones which have a direct line to emergency services. There are precinct (district) police stations all over the city. To find the nearest, dial *(212) 374 8000*.

Post Office

Stamps can be purchased in shops, supermarkets, and at hotel reception desks. Post offices are scattered throughout the city, with the main branch at Eighth Avenue/33rd Street on the West Side (*tel: (212) 967 8585*). It is open 24 hours a day, Monday to Saturday. Poste Restante ('c/o General Delivery' is the American term) should be addressed to the General Post Office, 321 Eighth Avenue, NY 10001. Two forms of identification need to be produced when collecting mail.

The police truck is designed to cope with big-city traffic

Public Transport

Contact the NYC Transit Authority Information Bureau (*tel: (718) 330 1234*), which is available 24 hours a day for transport information. Maps are available from the information booth at Grand Central Station or the New York Convention and Visitors' Bureau at 2 Columbus Circle.

Bus

About 40 services run in Manhattan, mostly running north-south along the avenues, with crosstown (east-west) services every 10 blocks or so. Bus stops are indicated by red, white, and blue poles marked with route numbers. Enter at the front and pay a flat fare; drop the exact money or subway token into the fare box. If you need to change buses, ask the driver for a free Addfare ticket.

Subway

Despite its reputation (no longer entirely deserved), the subway is the best way to get around New York. Express trains 'leapfrog' several stations at a time, while 'locals' stop at each one. A route map is displayed in each carriage and can also be easily obtained free of charge by request at any subway token booth. Passengers buy tokens and drop one into the turnstile to gain access to trains. You can also obtain discounted daily, weekly, monthly, or pay-per-ride Metrocards at token booths or vending machines at subway stations. These cards generally provide the easiest and cheapest way to travel via city buses and subways.

Taxis

Hail or wave when you see a cab displaying an illuminated 'available' sign. Fares are metered, with surcharges for weekend and night-time trips.

Trains

Amtrak (*tel: (212) 763 4545* or *1 800/872 7245 toll free*) serves stations to the north and south of the city from both Grand Central and Penn stations. The Long Island Railroad (*tel: (718) 217 LIRR*) serves destinations in Queens, and both the north and south shores of Long Island from Penn Station. Port Authority Trans-Hudson (PATH) provides commuter services to Newark, Jersey City, and Hoboken in New Jersey from stations in Manhattan (*tel: (800) 234 7284*). The Thomas Cook Overseas Timetable provides details of local and intercity trains, as well as long-distance buses.

Senior Citizens

Many hotels offer discounts of up to 50 per cent off rack rates, and most of New York City's top visitor attractions have special rates and services for seniors.

Student and Youth Travel

Students can get discounts in many attractions, but will need to show proof of their status. *(For YMCA and hostel details, see p176.)*

Telephones

Anywhere outside the 212 code area – Manhattan – is a long-distance call. The other boroughs are in the 718 area. Most phone booths take quarters, and a local call costs 25 cents for the first three minutes. For anything other than a local call dial 1, then the area code. For overseas calls dial 011 then the country code, followed by the local code without the initial zero, and finally the local number. *(Continued on p190.)*

Driving near Central Park

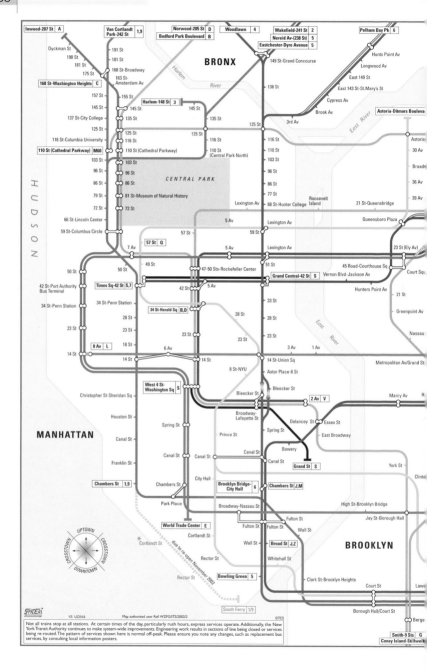

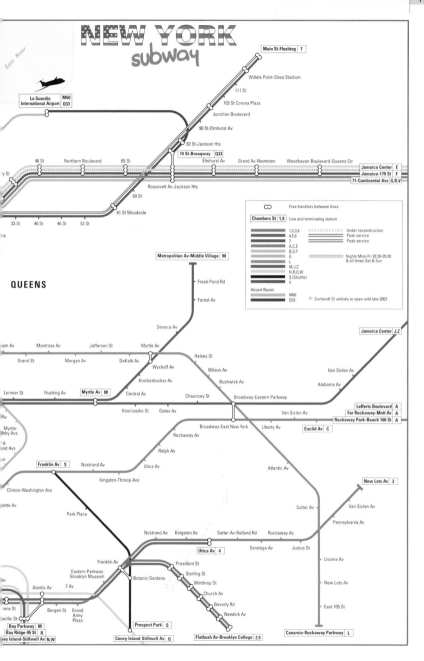

NEW YORK subway

East River

Main St-Flushing | 7

Willets Point-Shea Stadium

111 St

La Guardia International Airport | M60 | Q33

103 St Corona Plaza

Junction Boulevard

90 St-Elmhurst Av

82 St-Jackson Hts

74 St-Broaqway | Q33

Elmhurst Av   Grand Av-Newtown   Woodhaven Boulevard-Queens Ctr

Jamaica Center | E
Jamaica-179 St | F
71-Continental Avs | G,R,V

46 St   Northern Boulevard   65 St

y St

Roosevelt Av-Jackson Hts

69 St

33 St   40 St   46 St   52 St

61 St Woodside

ra

∞ Free transfers between lines

Chambers St | 1,9   Line and terminating station

1,2,3,9	▦▦▦ Under reconstruction
4,5,6	Peak service
7	Peak service
A,C,E	
B,D,F	
G	▨▨▨ Nights Mon-Fri 20.30-05.00
L	& all times Sat & Sun
M,J,Z	
N,R,Q,W	
S (Shuttle)	
V	

Airport Buses

M60
Q33

✳ Cortlandt St unlikely to open until late 2003

Metropolitan Av-Middle Village | M

Fresh Pond Rd

QUEENS

Forest Av

Seneca Av

Jamaica Center | J,Z

am Av   Montrose Av   Jefferson St   Myrtle Av

Grand St   Morgan Av   DeKalb Av   Halsey St   Van Siclen Av

Wyckoff Av   Wilson Av   Alabama Av

Lorimer St   Flushing Av   Myrtle Av | M   Knickerbocker Av   Bushwick Av

Central Av   Chauncey St   Broadway-Eastern Parkway

Lefferts Boulevard | A
Far Rockaway-Mott Av | A
Rockaway Park-Beach 166 St | A

Kosciuszko St   Gates Av   Van Siclen Av

Myrtle-
hby Avs

Broadway-East New York   Liberty Av   Euclid Av | C

rd-
and Avs

Rockaway Av

Ralph Av

Franklin Av | S   Nostrand Av   Utica Av   Atlantic Av

New Lots Av | 3

Clinton-Washington Avs

Kingston-Throop Avs

rette Av

Sutter Av   Van Siclen Av

Park Place

Pennsylvania Av

Nostrand Av   Kingston Av   Sutter Av-Rutland Rd   Rockaway Av

Utica Av | 4   Saratoga Av   Junius St

Livonia Av

Franklin Av   President St

Eastern Parkway
Brooklyn Museum

Sterling St

New Lots Av

y   Botanic Gardens   Winthrop St

Alantic Av   7 Av   Church St

East 105 St

vins St   Bergen St   Grand
Army
Plaza

Beverly Rd

Newkirk Av

Bay Parkway | M
Bay Ridge-95 St | R
ey Island-Stillwell Av | N,W

Prospect Park | S

Coney Island-Stillwell Av | Q

Flatbush Av-Brooklyn College | 2,5

Canarsie-Rockaway Parkway | L

Country codes:
Australia *61* **Canada** *1*
Eire *353* **New Zealand** *64*
UK *44*
For information on international
dialling, phone the toll-free number
1/800/874 4000. For directory inquiries
in New York dial *411*.

Thomas Cook

Branches of Thomas Cook Foreign
Exchange in New York change foreign
currency and Thomas Cook traveller's
cheques (free of commission), and
provide emergency assistance in the
event of loss or theft of Thomas Cook
traveller's cheques or MasterCard cards.
The city centre branches also offer
Moneygram, a fast international money
transfer service.
29 Broadway/Morris St (*tel: (212) 363
6206*). Open Mon–Fri 8.30am–4.30pm.
Herald Square, 1271 Broadway/32nd St
(*tel: (212) 679 4877*). Open Mon–Sat
9am–6.30pm, Sun 9am–5pm.
Times Square, 1590 Broadway/48th St
(*tel: (212) 265 6063*). Open Mon–Sat
9am–7pm (8pm Sun).
Grand Central, 317 Madison Ave/
42nd St (*tel: (212) 883 0401*).
Open Mon–Sat 9am–5pm.
511 Madison Ave/53rd St
(*tel: (212) 753 2595*). Open Mon–Sat
9am–7pm (5pm Sun).
For more information call *800 287 7362*;
or see *www.us.thomascook.com*

Tipping

Cab drivers now expect a few dollars
more than the fare, waiters and
waitresses should get 15 per cent
minimum, and hotel porters $1 for a
bag or two, more in proportion.

Travellers with Disabilities

Public buildings, sidewalks, and buses
(the newer ones, at least) have all been
modified to accommodate wheelchairs.
But the subway and most taxis remain
no-go areas for visitors with disabilities.
Information can be obtained from the
Center for the Handicapped, 52
Chambers Street (*tel: (212) 788 2830*).
For reduced fares, call NYC Transit's
Travel Line for People with Disabilities
(*tel: (718) 596 8585*). For door-to-door
services, call Access a Ride
(*tel: (877) 337 2017*).

The New York Division of Tourism,
1 Commerce Plaza, Albany, NY 12245
(*tel: (518) 474 4116* or *(800) 225 5697*),
and the New York State Parks
Department, Albany, NY 12238
(*tel (518) 474 0456*) provide information
on facilities for the disabled.

A breathtaking view from the Empire State
Building

ACKNOWLEDGEMENTS

The Automobile Association wishes to thank the following organizations, libraries and photographers for their assistance in the preparation of this book.

ALLSPORT 152, 153, 156a, 157a, 157b
CHRISTINE PEMBERTON 98a
JYOTI M BANERJEE 79
MARY EVANS PICTURE LIBRARY 124a, 124b, 125a, 125b
NEIL SETCHFIELD 3, 7, 26b, 28, 34b, 49, 52, 67, 68, 78, 83, 86, 92a, 106b, 141, 171
NYC & COMPANY - The Convention & Visitors Bureau back cover top left, back cover top centre, back cover centre, spine, 2, 5, 6, 8, 11, 16, 24, 25b, 27, 34a, 35a, 36, 39b, 44, 50, 60, 69, 76, 89, 99a, 99b, 104, 105, 109, 120, 122, 123, 127a, 127b, 128, 129, 142, 144, 154, 156b, 166
PICTURES COLOUR LIBRARY 17a, 43, 85, 93, 116, 137
SPECTRUM COLOUR LIBRARY 88a

The remaining pictures are held in the AA PHOTO LIBRARY and were taken by PAUL KENWARD, with the exception of pages back cover top right, 15, 20, 26a, 32, 33b, 35b, 40, 61, 62, 63, 65a, 71, 75, 77a, 100, 101, 103, 112, 113a, 113b, 132, 148, 149, 163a, 168a, 168b, 169b, 172, 173, 175, 176b, 177 (DOUGLAS CORRANCE); 170 (ANTONY SOUTER).

FOR LABURNUM TECHNOLOGIES

Design Director	Alpana Khare	**Photo Editor**	Radhika Singh
Series Director	Razia Grover	**DTP Designers**	Neeraj Aggarwal
Editors	Madhumadhavi Singh		Harish Aggarwal
	Rajiv Jayaram, Deepshikha Singh		

Updating and additional research on this edition was done by Ria Patel and Mytri Singh.
Thanks to Marie Lorimer for the Index.